New & Selected

THINGS TAKING PLACE

Books by May Swenson

THINGS TAKING PLACE

ICONOGRAPHS

HALF SUN HALF SLEEP

TO MIX WITH TIME

A CAGE OF SPINES

ANOTHER ANIMAL

For Children

POEMS TO SOLVE

MORE POEMS TO SOLVE

THE GUESS & SPELL COLORING BOOK

Translation

TOMAS TRANSTRÖMER: WINDOWS & STONES

New & Selected
THINGS TAKING PLACE

Poems by MAY SWENSON

An Atlantic Monthly Press Book

LITTLE, BROWN AND COMPANY • BOSTON • TORONTO

FIRST EDITION
T 11/78

Library of Congress Cataloging in Publication Data

Swenson, May.
    New & selected things taking place.

    "An Atlantic Monthly Press book."
    Includes index.
    I. Title.
PS3537.W4786N4   811'.5'4   78–16671
ISBN 0–316–82520–4
ISBN 0–316–82521–2 pbk.

ATLANTIC–LITTLE, BROWN BOOKS
ARE PUBLISHED BY
LITTLE, BROWN AND COMPANY
IN ASSOCIATION WITH
THE ATLANTIC MONTHLY PRESS

Published simultaneously in Canada
by Little, Brown & Company (Canada) Limited

PRINTED IN THE UNITED STATES OF AMERICA

Some of the new poems, sections I and II of *Things Taking Place,* have been previously published in the following: *American Poetry Review, American Review, Antaeus* ("First Walk on the Moon"), *The Atlantic Monthly, Carleton Miscellany, Chelsea* ("O'Keeffe Retrospective"), *Chicago Tribune Magazine, Cornell Review, First Stone, Greensboro Review* ("Cold Colors" and "Shu Swamp, Spring" under the title "Easter"), *Harper's, The Little Magazine, Maryland Poetry Review, Modern Occasions, The Nation, The New Yorker* ("Speed," "Staying at Ed's Place," "On Addy Road," "Running on the Shore," "September Things," "October," "November Night," "View to the North," and "The Pure Suit of Happiness"), *Paintbrush, Paumanok Rising, Place, Poetry* ("Digging in the Garden . . . ," "Ending," "Fashion in the 70's," "Going to the Whitney and Walking on the Floor," "July 4th"), *Poetry Northwest* ("Dream After Nanook"), *Pomegranate Press Broad side* ("Birthday" under the title "Questions/Answers"), *Quartet* ("Today"), *Saturday Review, The Scribner Anthology of Children's Literature, Shenandoah.*

"The Thickening Mat" and "Teleology" © 1971 by The New York Times Company. Reprinted by permission.

New Poems in THINGS TAKING PLACE I & II
are for R.R.K.

Contents

II

THINGS TAKING PLACE

I

A NAVAJO BLANKET

Eye-dazzlers the Indians weave. Three colors
are paths that pull you in, and pin you
to the maze. Brightness makes your eyes jump,
surveying the geometric field. Alight, and enter
any of the gates—of Blue, of Red, of Black.
Be calmed and hooded, a hawk brought down,
glad to fasten to the forearm of a Chief.

You can sleep at the center,
attended by Sun that never fades, by Moon
that cools. Then, slipping free of zigzag and
hypnotic diamond, find your way out
by the spirit trail, a faint Green thread that
secretly crosses the border, where your mind
is rinsed and returned to you like a white cup.

BISON CROSSING NEAR MT. RUSHMORE

There is our herd of cars stopped,
staring respectfully at the line of bison crossing.
One big-fronted bull nudges his cow into a run.
She and her calf are first to cross.
In swift dignity the dark-coated caravan sweeps through
the gap our cars leave in the two-way stall
on the road to the Presidents.
The polygamous bulls guarding their families from the rear,
the honey-brown calves trotting head-to-hip
by their mothers—who are lean and muscled as bulls,
with chin tassels and curved horns—
all leap the road like a river, and run.
The strong and somber remnant of western freedom
disappears into the rough grass of the draw,
around the point of the mountain.
The bison, orderly, disciplined by the prophet-faced,
heavy-headed fathers, threading the pass
of our awestruck stationwagons, airstreams and trailers,
if in dread of us give no sign,
go where their leaders twine them, over the prairie.
And we keep to our line,
staring, stirring, revving idling motors, moving
each behind the other, herdlike, where the highway leads.

SPEED
Winnipeg to Medicine Hat, Manitoba, Canada

In 200 miles
a tender painting
on the wind-

shield, not yet done,
in greeny yellows,
crystalline pinks,

a few smeared
browns. Fuselages
split on impact,

stuck, their juices
instantly dried. Spat-
tered flat out-

lines, superfine
strokes, tokens of
themselves flying,

frail engines
died in various
designs: mainly arrow-

shapes, wings gone,
bellies smitten
open, glaze and tincture

the wipers can't
erase. In 400 miles
a palette, thick

impasto; in 600
a palimpsest the sun
bakes through. Stained

glass, not yet done
smiting the wind-
borne, speeds on.

THE NORTH RIM

Great dark bodies, the mountains.
Between them wriggling the canyon road,
little car, bug-eyed, beaming, goes
past ticking and snicking of August insects,
smell of sage and cedar, to a summit of stars.
Sky glints like fluorescent rock.
Cloth igloo erected, we huff up our bed,
listen to the quaking of leaf-hearts
that, myriad, shadow our sleep.

At dawn, the bodies discovered rugged, oblate,
Indian-warpaint-red, a rooster crows.
Barefoot in brickdust, we strike our tent.
Car crawls the knee of the Great White Throne.
Chiseled by giant tomahawks, the slabs.
In half-finished doorways broad gods stand.
Wind-whipped from the niches, white-throated swifts
razor the void.
We rise to ponderosa, to deer park, to moraine,
mountain bluebirds stippling the meadows,
and coast to the Grand Rim:

Angular eels of light
scribble among the buttes and crinoline
escarpments. Thunder's organ tumbles
into the stairwell of the gorge.
When rain and mist divide their veil,
westering sun, a palette knife, shoves into the cut
colors thick and bright, enclabbering
every serrate slant and vertical;
hard edged, they jut forward,
behind, beside them purple groins and pits
in shadow. Shadow within shadow beneath a shawl
of shadow darkens, and we dare not blink
till light tweaks out.

Morning at Cape Royal. A Merry-Go-Round
out there in the red cirque, Brahma's Temple.
Many Pavilions make a Great
                              Pavilion.
                        Where mountain
                  peaks eroded to flat
            ranges, flat ranges broke
         and parted, became pediments,
            and pointed pediments, pinnacles, were
         honed to skinny minarets,
or else, inverted cones, big-headed totems—
Look: On the slope a stone Boot two miles high,
the hip-end slouched in folds, some seven-leaguer
left six million years.
A lizard where I sit, with petrific eye,
is Dinosaur's little cousin
watching me from Juniper's bony root.

Two coils of the river seen from here,
muddy infinite oozing heavy paint.
Each object has its shadow. Or, if not,
must vanish. Now while the sun leans,
tabernacles form. Allow dark openings,
violet-cool arcades. Establish bases,
though colosseums, carved by the shift
of a cloud, descend pendant,
and Great sinks into shadow.
We must go. It rains. The car trickles east
over the frogback of the Kaibab Forest.
I must imagine morning, from Angel's Window
how to dive, firebrushed by the sun.

CAMPING IN MADERA CANYON

We put up our tent while the dark closed in
and thickened, the road a black trough
winding the mountain down. Leaving the lantern
ready to light on the stone table,
we took our walk. The sky was a bloom
of sharp-petaled stars.

Walls of the woods, opaque and still,
gave no light or breath or echo, until,
faint and far, a string of small toots—
nine descending notes—the whiskered owl's
signal. A tense pause . . . then, his mate's
identical reply.

At the canyon's foot, we turned,
climbed back to camp, between tall walls
of silent dark. Snugged deep into our sacks,
so only noses felt the mountain chill,
we heard the owls once more. Farther from us,
but closer to each other. The pause, that linked
his motion with her seconding, grew longer
as we drowsed. Then, expectation frayed,
we forgot to listen, slept.

In a tent, first light tickles the skin
like a straw. Still freezing cold out there,
but we in our pouches sense the immense
volcano, sun, about to pour
gold lava over the mountain, upon us.
Wriggling out, we sleepily unhinge,
make scalding coffee, shivering, stand and sip;
tin rims burn our lips.

Daybirds wake, the woods are filling
with their rehearsal flutes and pluckings,
buzzes, scales and trills. Binoculars
dangling from our necks, we walk
down the morning road. Rooms of the woods

stand open. Glittering trunks
rise to a limitless loft of blue. New snow,
a delicate rebozo, drapes the peak that,
last night, stooped in heavy shadow.

Night hid this day. What sunrise may it be
the dark to? What wider light ripens to dawn
behind familiar light? As by encircling arms
our backs are warmed by the blessing sun,
all is revealed and brought to feature.
All but the owls. The Apaches believe
them ghosts of ancestors, who build their nests
of light with straws pulled from the sun.

The whiskered owls are here, close by,
in the tops of the pines, invisible and radiant,
as we, blind and numb, awaken—our just-born
eyes and ears, our feet that walk—
as brightness bathes the road.

BRONCO BUSTING, EVENT #1

The stall so tight he can't raise heels or knees
when the cowboy, coccyx to bareback, touches down

tender as a deerfly, forks him, gripping the rope-
handle over the withers, testing the cinch,

as if hired to lift a cumbersome piece of brown
luggage, while assistants perched on the rails arrange

the kicker, a foam-rubber band around the narrowest,
most ticklish part of the loins, leaning full weight

on neck and rump to keep him throttled, this horse,
"Firecracker," jacked out of the box through the sprung

gate, in the same second raked both sides of the belly
by ratchets on booted heels, bursts into five-way

motion: bucks, pitches, swivels, humps, and twists,
an all-over-body-sneeze that must repeat

until the flapping bony lump attached to his spine is gone.
A horn squawks. From the dust gets up a buster named Tucson.

ST. AUGUSTINE-BY-THE-SEA

1

A sullen morning.
A long string,
with knots in it,
being pulled,
pelicans fly,
follow the leader
in fog, their line
the only horizon.
When the measuring
string is lost,
sea becomes sky.

2

Peak tide.
Ocean trying
to bury the land
again, again
slaughters
the surf-pierced
reefs, grinding
coarse, sifting
fine, the sand
salmon, like flesh.

3

On reddish sand
by the coquina
cliffs, noon sun
swallows my body.
I lie in the mouth
of a cannibal flower.
Wave after hissing
wave, the cold sea
climbs to me
to douse with green
glaze and fizz white,
the fiery flower's
appetite.

ONE OF THE STRANGEST

Stuffed pink stocking, the neck,
toe of pointed black, the angled beak,
thick heel with round eye in it upside down, the pate,

swivels, dabbles, skims the soup of pond all day
for small meat. That split polished toe is mouth
of the wading flamingo

whose stilts, the rosy knee joints, bend
the wrong way. When planted
on one straight stem, a big fluffy flower

is body a pink leg, wrung, lifts up over,
lays an awkward shoe to sleep on top of,
between flocculent elbows, the soft peony wings.

LAST NIGHT AT LONG PINE

Up and walking, 3:30 A.M., under the Southern Cross.
My horsehide jacket squeaks. It's dark on the path.
Is someone behind me? No, it's my shadow.

Bullfrogs whickering, splash of a night-diving duck.
My cigarette's ember to sticks of a fire
winks in the sleeping camp.

A far train bawls at a crossing. Mournful phantom
animal: "Of metal, when shall I mate?"

We strike at sunup, begin the struggle toward cold
incarnation in the North. From soft nights too soon
exiled under smaller, sharper, scantier stars.

FROM SEA CLIFF, MARCH

The water's wide spread
(it is storm gray)
following the border of the far shore ahead,
leads the eye south,
tucks into a cove
where, at the point of another line of hills,
big rocks like huts
strung along the flats
are embraced by the sliding
long arms of the tide.
A red buoy bangs (but you can't hear it,
size of a golf tee seen from here),
wind is picking up, cleats of the water
rising and deepening, no white ridges yet.

In the cove's corner
on an island by itself,
an intricate old house,
set on a rock shelf
beside a lighthouse, saltcellar shaped,
with a round silvery top,
pokes up alone in the wind's main way.
Old house, of many chimneys, dormers and decks,
doll-sized, of clapboard, is outlined plain
at the farthest string of sight,
perched under swirling specks of white
gulls against gray
wide water, lowering sky
shutting down the distance under wind and rain.

OLD NO. 1

A shock to find you washed up on the beach,
old No. 1, looking like an iron whale,
or a blunt rocket. What a storm it took

to pull you from bottom, breaking the root
of the anchor. And what a wave, to roll
your solid ton, like a giant's thick and broken

pencil point, so far up the scoured beach.
You're dumped on a ridge of sedge the storm tide
harvested, big ring in your snout half buried,

rusted cone below your watermark scabby orange,
glazed black paintskin of belly and round
tabled top fouled with dull white gull droppings.

But you're still No. 1—it's clearly stenciled
upon you—old Stove Pipe, old Opera Hat,
Bouncer in the Channel, Policeman of the Bay

all boats salute. Your colleague, nipple-headed
Big Red, No. 2, is out there swaying on today's
gentler tide like a jolly bottle, but

you, Black Butt, you're gone aground, down
past the count of ten, with a frowzy dead gull
upended in the sandy litter by your side.

SHU SWAMP, SPRING

Young skunk
cabbages all over
the swamp.

Brownish purple,
yellow-specked
short tusks,

they thicken,
twirl and point
like thumbs.

Thumbs of old
gloves, the nails
poked through

and curled.
By Easter, fingers
will have flipped out

fat and green,
Old gloves, brown
underground,

the seams split.
The nails
have been growing.

ON THE EDGE

I was thinking, while I was working on my income tax,
here in the open angle of a V—
that blue on the map that's water—my house
tucked into the fold of a hill, on the edge
of a ragged beak of the sea
that widens and narrows according to the tide:
"This little house will be swallowed some year.
Not yet. But threatened."

Chips are houses, twigs are trees
on the woodland ledges along the lip,
the blue throat open, thirsty. Where my chip-roof sits,
sandland loosens, boulders shift downslope,
bared roots of old trunks stumble.
The undermining and undulating lurch
is all one way, the shore dragged south
to spill into and fill another mouth.

I was thinking while I was working: "The April sun
is warm." Suddenly, all the twigs on the privet
budded green, the cardinal flamed and called,
the maple rained its flowerets down
and spread leaf-grown. July's plush roses bloomed,
were blown. A hundred gladioli sunsets in a row
raced to die, and dyed the cove,
while the sea crawled the sand, gnawed on the cliff.

And leisurely, cracks in the flagstones happened,
leaks in the roof. The gateposts crumbled,
mortar in the stone wall loosened,
boards in the porch let the nailheads through.
I was thinking, while April's crocus
poked out of earth on the cesspool top:
"Blueblack winter of water coming—icewhite, rockhard
tide will be pounding the side of the gaping V. . . .

"But smell of the windfresh, salty morning,
flash of the sunwhipped beak of the sea!
Better get last year's layers of old leaves up,
before this year's green bursts out, turns brown,
comes blowing down," I was thinking
while I was working on my income tax.

PAINTING THE GATE

I painted the mailbox. That was fun.
I painted it postal blue.
Then I painted the gate.
I painted a spider that got on the gate.
I painted his mate.
I painted the ivy around the gate.
Some stones I painted blue,
and part of the cat as he rubbed by.
I painted my hair. I painted my shoe.
I painted the slats, both front and back,
all their beveled edges, too.
I painted the numbers on the gate—
I shouldn't have, but it was too late.
I painted the posts, each side and top,
I painted the hinges, the handle, the lock,
several ants and a moth asleep in a crack.
At last I was through.
I'd painted the gate
shut, me out, with both hands dark blue,
as well as my nose, which,
early on, because of a sudden itch,
got painted. But wait!
I had painted the gate.

WRITTEN WHILE RIDING THE LONG ISLAND
RAIL ROAD

Hard water and square wheels.
A foot wears a hat and walks on its thumbs.
The clouds are of plaster. That hiss is a box.
Honey is hairy. This cipher's a house.
In a coffin of chocolate the hatchet is laid.
A cactus is sneezing. A blind violin
has digested a penny. The telephone's juice
has stiffened a horsefly, whose porcelain curse
is rocking the corridor. Pockets are born,
but the stubble of rainbows cannot be controlled.
The bite of the barber begins to compete
with the weight of a capsized spondee or stilt.
The chime of the calendar suffers from rust,
and cobalt is scorched beyond closure or froth.
If a portion of pinch is applied to a cube,
and scissorlike bubbles produced with a switch,
we can burnish the windows with faucets and lips.
Will oral implosions enrapture the fish
so that their lecterns, transparently diced,
while diploid, will dapple? We tried it, and found
that a petrified lace leaked out of the pistol
of Charlotte, the Kink, while Pug, drunk on lightning,
slept in the bank with ankles and rabbits
he'd slaughtered with borscht. Snafu just sucked
on his pommel and barfed. Then let the moon's
carpet display a cartoon: The lawn's perpendicular,
Daddy comes home, and the doorknob's a funnel.
An owl's in the sink. There's a flag in the oven.
The front page is blank.

APPOINTMENT IN NEW YORK

At 42nd Street, finding the Library Lions
crouched in raw wood boxes with plastic-sheeted
sides. . . . "Are To Be Cleaned," a sign says. . . .
The two grand heads, as if behind the fog
of oxygen tents . . . their haughty nostrils
unable to breathe the dirty air.

In Charleston, S.C., says the *Times,*
they're putting diapers of black plastic on
the old cab horses that drive tourists through
historic streets. Poor trussed-into-harness
beasts, blindered and rubber-shod, endure a new
indignity: not only nose bags, but ass bags.

In Disney World in Florida, white-overalled
attendants run behind the Percherons
pulling the fake red and gold stagecoach,
with scoop and brush take up the steaming buns
that fall on waxed and polished pavement. . . .

All filth there whisked away. . . . Dare to drop
a gum wrapper, it's gone—instantly speared
into a white enameled barrel trundled on wheels.
The street is like a room. Perfection
is maintained in the Fun House, too.

STAYING AT ED'S PLACE

I like being in your apartment, and not disturbing anything.
As in the woods I wouldn't want to move a tree,
or change the play of sun and shadow on the ground.

The yellow kitchen stool belongs right there
against white plaster. I haven't used your purple towel
because I like the accidental cleft of shade you left in it.

At your small six-sided table, covered with mysterious
dents in the wood like a dartboard, I drink my coffee
from your brown mug. I look into the clearing

of your high front room, where sunlight slopes through bare
window squares. Your Afghanistan hammock, a man-sized cocoon
slung from wall to wall, your narrow desk and typewriter

are the only furniture. Each morning your light from the east
douses me where, with folded legs, I sit in your meadow,
a casual spread of brilliant carpets. Like a cat or dog

I take a roll, then, stretched out flat
in the center of color and pattern, I listen
to the remote growl of trucks over cobbles on Bethune Street below.

When I open my eyes I discover the peaceful blank
of the ceiling. Its old paint-layered surface is moonwhite
and trackless, like the Sea—of Tranquillity.

FASHION IN THE 70'S

Like, everyone wants to look black
in New York these days.
Faces with black lenses, black
frames around the eyes,
faces framed in black
beards. Afros on all the blacks—
beautiful. But like,
everyone looks puff-headed.
Slouching along in black
leather, fake fur, sleazy body-
shirts, floppy pants, wearing black
boots with thick heels. Bootblacks
have disappeared. Good—but like,
everyone wants to look hoody.
Blacks used to want to look
white. And whites used to want
to be pink. That's pig now.
Sharp, neat, crewcut, cleancut,
blonds preferred is out. O.K., but
whites, the women especially,
if they don't want to look black,
want to look dead. Like,
morticians make them up,
in the Ugly Parlors.
Blacks are loose walkers,
relaxed, laughing. For whites
it's hip to look uptight, scowl,
be grimy, wear scary, puffed-out hair.
Crowds of square-toed black
boots, heavy heels crossing the Walk-
Don't-Walk streets. Like, everyone
wants to look ugly in New York
these days. Like, ugly is beautiful.

GOING TO THE WHITNEY AND WALKING ON THE FLOOR

There were things that looked like part of the floor
    or part of the wall or the ceiling.
Some ceiling things were on the walls.
Some wall things were on the floor.
No things were on the ceiling that weren't part of
      the ceiling, but some floor things that looked like
      they belonged on the floor reflected some of the ceiling:

A small swimming pool, for instance,
    or the model for one,
    only the rim enameled red.
A little boy's mother said,
    "Don't touch anything."
An out-of-kilter rectangle
    mounted on one of its corners was strung,
    it seemed, with thick wire, so made you think of a harp,
    for instance, by Arp.
But it had rungs
    of wood when you stood
    closer. The little boy would
    have liked to crawl
    through all
    the squares of an aluminum tunnel, but a guard stood
    there. On the wall
    a framed drawing showed the building plan
    for four squares, four-by-four,
    or
    four-square, labeled, UNTITLED #4 = 4 SQUARES 4 X 4—
ALUMINUM, PENCIL ON PAPER. This was printed on the card.
I wanted very much to add, UNDER GLASS—MOUNTED ON WALL,
    PLASTER, but it was under glass, and I didn't have
    a pencil and, anyway, a guard
    was standing near.
While I waited
    for him to notice how my face controlled a sneer,
    some schoolchildren, disgorged by the elevator,

into what might appear
to be a playroom, were momentarily elated,
but quickly wilted when, on spreading through the space,
they discovered all the bright
blocks or transparent boxes had the same
name,
namely, UNTITLED,
and weren't meant
to be entered
or climbed upon or used in any way,
except for them to stand
and stare.

Some of the things there
would have made a fine sound if kicked
or drummed upon. Others, it was apparent,
were transparent,
being lit from within as if to make
you look for a snake,
or sleepy puppy, but contained
nothing, really, just a color
such as frozen yellow
Jell-O,
or lemon juice jars cubed,
cracked here and there, so that all the juice had drained.

There were long narrow tubed
things along the walls, like shelves in a post office
or bank,
that had set-in sections you could look through
like a periscope. Although no prank
was intended, nothing was disclosed at the far end,
unless another eye, of someone trying to find out
what it was all about,
happened to appear from that end.

The children giggled and scoffed in whispers,
when sufficiently far away from their teacher, who,
regarding the guard in a guarded way,

was too
   timid to ask him something. A boy,
   who was with his girl, covertly touched
   a placard lettered DO NOT TOUCH, and snatched
   back his finger and sucked it, as if it were burnt,
   and the girl laughed.
Having circled the objects on the floor once, and consulted
      their identical titles, all of them UNTITLED,
      but with different dates,
      the children collected at the elevator
      which sucked them in, and away.

In the silent room like a play-
      room, I began to enjoy the floor.
The rough stone squares against the flat
      soles of my shoes that
      allowed a rhythmic scrape and snick wherever
      I walked, gave back an echo bare
      and dungeonlike.
I paced,
      touching
      the floor intimately with each
      step, happy alone,
      noticing each pave-stone,
      its individual quarry marks and whittles.
I circled each of the three guards,
      standing
      suspenseful as if below a gibbet.
I paid each the attention worthy of his exhibit.
Their gray
      suits were as gray as the play-
      room stones. In a far corner on the white
      wall, I found a little sculpture I might
      have missed, had I not been aware:
A cranberry
      red
      boxlike thing, perhaps of lead,
      or other heavy metal, cleverly nicked
      to appear utilitarian,

with a glass insert through which could be seen—
        but it was locked in—a brass
        handle.
The placard giving the date wasn't there, but this
        three-dimensional construction unaccountably was titled
        by a raised insignia worked into the medium itself:
        PULL TO SET OFF ALARM.
It made a little shelf
        on the wall. I told a guard
        its card
        was missing, but that I thought it was
        the best in show.
No.
I didn't. I only thought of telling him so,
        as he looked at his watch, said it was closing
        time, told me to go.

O'KEEFFE RETROSPECTIVE

Into the sacral cavity can fit the skull of a deer,
the vertical pleat in the snout, place of the yoni.
Within the embrasure of antlers that flare, sensitive
tips like fingers defining thighs and hips, inner horns
hold ovary curls of space.

Where a white bead rolls at the fulcrum of widening knees,
black dawn evolves, a circular saw of polished speed;
its bud, like Mercury, mad in its whiz, shines, although
stone jaws of the same delta, opposite, lock agape—
blunt monolithic hinge, stranded, grand, tide gone out.

A common boundary has hip and hill, sky and pelvic basin.
From the upright cleft, shadow-entwirled, early veils
of spectral color—a tender maypole, girlish, shy, unbraids
to rainbow streams slowly separated.

A narrow eye on end, the lily's riper crack of bloom:
stamen stiff, it lengthens, swells, at its ball (walled pupil)
a sticky tear of sap. Shuttlecock (divided muzzle of the dried
deer's face, eyeholes outline the ischium) is, in the flap of
the jack-in-the-pulpit, silken flesh. As windfolds of
the mesa (regal, opulent odalisque) are, saturate orange, sunset.

Cerulean is solid. Clouds are tiles, or floats of ice
a cobalt spa melts. Evaporating, they yet grip their shapes;
if walked on, prove not fluff and steam. These clouds
are hard. Then rock may be pillow, stones vacant spaces.
Look into the hole: it will bulk. Hold the rock: it will empty.

Opposite, the thousand labia of a gray rose puff apart,
like smoke, yet they have a fixed, or nearly fixed, union,
skeletal, innominate, but potent to implode, flush red,
tighten to a first bud-knot, single, sacral.
Not quite closed, the cruciform fissure in the deer's
nose bone, symphysis of the pubis.

Where inbetweens turn visible blues, white objects vanish,
except—see, high at horizon on a vast canvas sky—
one undisciplined tuft, little live cloud, blowing:
fleece, breath of illusion.

POET TO TIGER

The Hair
You went downstairs
saw a hair in the sink
and squeezed my toothpaste by the neck.
You roared. My ribs are sore.
This morning even my pencil's got your toothmarks.
Big Cat Eye cocked on me you see bird bones.
Snuggled in the rug of your belly
your breath so warm
I smell delicious fear.
Come breathe on me rough pard
put soft paws here.

The Salt
You don't put salt on anything
so I'm eating without.
Honey on the eggs is all right
mustard on the toast.
I'm not complaining I'm saying I'm
living with *you*.
You like your meat raw
don't care if it's cold.
Your stomach must have tastebuds
you swallow so fast.
Night falls early. It's foggy. Just now

I found another of your bite marks in the cheese.
I'm hungry. Please
come bounding home
I'll hand you the wine to open
with your teeth.
Scorch me a steak unsalted
boil my coffee twice

say the blessing to a jingle on the blue TV.
Under the lap robe on our chilly couch

look behind my ears "for welps"
and hug me.

The Sand
You're right I brought a grain
or two of sand
into bed I guess in my socks.
But it was you pushed them off
along with everything else.

Asleep you flip
over roll
everything under
you and off
me. I'm always grabbing
for my share of the sheets.

Or else you wake me every hour with sudden
growled I-love-yous
trapping my face between those plushy
shoulders. All my float-dreams turn spins
and never finish. I'm thinner
now. My watch keeps running fast.
But best is when we're riding pillion
my hips within your lap. You let me steer.
Your hand and arm go clear
around my ribs your moist
dream teeth fastened on my nape.

A grain of sand in the bed upsets you or
a hair on the floor.
But you'll get
in slick and wet from the shower if I let
you. Or with your wool cap
and skiing jacket on
if it's cold.
Tiger don't scold me
don't make me comb my hair outdoors.

Cuff me careful. Lick don't
crunch. Make last what's yours.

The Dream
You get into the tub holding *The Naked Ape*
in your teeth. You wet that blond
three-cornered pelt lie back wide
chest afloat. You're reading
in the rising steam and I'm
drinking coffee from your tiger cup.
You say you dreamed
I had your baby book
and it was pink and blue.
I pointed to a page and there
was your face with a cub grin.

You put your paws in your armpits
make a tiger-moo.
Then you say: "Come here
Poet and take
this hair
off me." I do.
It's one of mine. I carefully
kill it and carry
it outside. And stamp on it
and bury it.

In the begonia bed.
And then take off my shoes
not to bring a grain
of sand in to get
into our bed.
I'm going to
do the cooking
now instead
of you.
And sneak some salt in
when you're not looking.

OVERBOARD

What throws you out is what drags you in

What drags you in is what throws you

What throws you out is what drags

What drags is what throws you

What throws you drags

What drags throws

Throws drag

Thrags

Drags throw

What throws drags

What drags you throws

What throws is what drags you

What drags you in is what throws

What throws you out is what drags you

What drags you in is what throws you out

What throws you in is what drags you

What drags you out is what throws

What throws you out drags you

What drags throws you in

What throws drags you

Drags throw you

Thrags

You give yourself such funny
                    looks
            when you
                    look
    in the mirror. You're
                        looking
    at yourself, but you're not
                        looking
            at yourself
                    looking.
                You
                    look
    at a pimple on your brow. You
            bare your teeth. I'm
                        looking
            at you
                        looking
    funny at yourself in the mirror.
                You're not
                        looking
            at me. I
                    look
            at you. I
                    look
        in the mirror at you
                        looking
    in the mirror. In the mirror I
                    look
            at me,
                        looking
            at you
                        looking
    at a pimple and baring your teeth.
                You don't
                    look
        at me in the mirror
                        looking
            at myself
                        looking
            at you
                        looking
    at a pimple on your brow.
        You give yourself funny
                    looks,
                not
                        looking
        at me in the mirror.
                        Look!
        I bare my teeth!

HOLDING THE TOWEL

You swam out
through the boats
your head an orange

buoy sun-daubed
bobbing. My squint
lost you to nibbling

waves. I looked
for a mast to tilt
to glint with your splash

but couldn't see
past the huddled boats.
I found round heads sun-red

dipping rising tipping.
They were tethered
floats. When you dove

from the stovepipe
buoy in the far
furrow of the channel

I was still
scanning the nearby
nowhere-going boats.

ANALYSIS OF BASEBALL

It's about
the ball,
the bat,
and the mitt.
Ball hits
bat, or it
hits mitt.
Bat doesn't
hit ball, bat
meets it.
Ball bounces
off bat, flies
air, or thuds
ground (dud)
or it
fits mitt.

Bat waits
for ball
to mate.
Ball hates
to take bat's
bait. Ball
flirts, bat's
late, don't
keep the date.
Ball goes in
(thwack) to mitt,
and goes out
(thwack) back
to mitt.

Ball fits
mitt, but
not all
the time.
Sometimes
ball gets hit
(pow) when bat
meets it,
and sails
to a place
where mitt
has to quit
in disgrace.
That's about
the bases
loaded,
about 40,000
fans exploded.

It's about
the ball,
the bat,
the mitt,
the bases
and the fans.
It's done
on a diamond,
and for fun.
It's about
home, and it's
about run.

WATCHING THE JETS LOSE TO BUFFALO AT SHEA

The feel of that leather baby
solid against your sternum,
you hug its skull and bottom
between huge huddled shoulders.
It's wrapped in your arms and wedged
under the hard muzzle
of your stuck-out faceguard.

Your thighs pumping, you run
to deliver the baby
to a cradle of grass at the goalposts.
But it's bumped from your arms,
and you're mounted
as if your back were leather.
Your legs cut away, you fold,

you tumble like a treetrunk.
Your brain's for the ground to split
like a leather egg, but it doesn't.
Your helmet takes the concussion.
Sent aloft by a leather toe,
a rugged leather baby
dropped from the sky and slammed

into the sling of your arms.
Oh, the feel of that leather bundle.
Oh, what a blooper and fumbler
you are, that you couldn't nest it,
that you lost and couldn't nurse it,
long enough to lay it
in a cradle of grass at the goalposts.

CHOOSING CRAFT

Striped equilateral sails,
the morning placid,
corners tugged trim,
jab for the belly of the wind.
Try to be accurate.
One tall, white isosceles spanks water,
helped by outboard motor,
canvas popping in a made breeze.
Put forth without effort.
Then expect, what neither gust
nor inertia will upset, to upset.
Let the wind pick up.
Tricorn scraps, as for a chance-built
quilt over the cove, scoot free.
How close-hauled, canted, apt to capsize
you keep, must be why you don't.

JULY 4TH

Gradual bud and bloom and seedfall speeded up
are these mute explosions in slow motion.

From vertical shoots above the sea, the fire
flowers open, shedding their petals.

Black waves, turned more than moonwhite, pink
ice, lightning blue, echo our gasps of admiration

as they crash and hush. Another bush ablaze
snicks straight up. A gap like heartstop between

the last vanished particle and the thuggish boom.
And the thuggish boom repeats in stutters

from sandhill hollows in the shore. We want
more. A twirling sun, or dismembered chrysanthemum

bulleted up, leisurely bursts, in an instant
timestreak is suckswooped back to its core.

And we want more: we want red giant, white dwarf,
black hole, extinct, orgasmic, all in one!

ON ADDY ROAD

A flicker with a broken neck
we found on the road, brought home, and laid
under a beech tree, liver-red the leaves.

On gaming-table green, in autumn shade,
we spread his yellow-shafted wing;
the spokes slid closed when we let go.

Splendid as the king
of spades, black half-moon under chin,
breast of speckled ermine,

scarlet ribbon at the nape—
how long before his raiment fade,
and gold slats tear within the cape?

We left him on the chilly grass.
Through the equinoctial night
we slept and dreamed

of the wetland meadow where,
one tawny dawn, the red fox crept—
an instant only, then his pelt

merged with the windbent reeds,
not to be seen again.
Next morning, going barefoot to the lawn,

we found the flicker's body gone, and saw
in the dew of the sandy road
faint print of a fox's paw.

ANGELS AT "UNSUBDUED"

All the angels are here this morning, in the striped light
and shade. Some—ruby-eyed, patterned black and tan and white—
are kicking leaves behind them, finding their food.
There are white-throated angels, scarlet-headed angels,
angels of shrill blue. Some bronzed angels are spangling wings
and dabbling iridescent heads in the rain pan.

On cleats down the trunk of a pine descends the downy angel. Her tiny
drill dithers faster than a snare drum. Black-capped or tufted,
round-eyed cherubs flick to ground, scrambling for thrown seed.
The bent-tailed, the brindled, the small red-breasted
next arrive, jab needle-beaks into the suet. Until a cocky
coal-winged angel with red patches elbows them off.

Neat-fronted in clerical gray, cat angels have quietly landed.
They raise their spread tails, flashing rusty coverts.
Rushing on high legs from under the thornbush, an arrogant brown
angel shrieks that he can thrash them all.

Now alights the crimson Pope of angels, masked, with thick
pink nose. He's trailed by two pale female acolytes,
ticking and ruffling crested crowns. Cracking two seeds,
the splendid seraph hops, as if on pogo stick, to each in turn,
to put between accepting beaks the sacrament—they stand agape
for this—an act that's like a kiss.

Yellow-throated angels loop to a wag of honeysuckle, waiting
for a gang of raucous purple angels to finish bathing and fly.
Still kicking leaves under the laurel, shy black-headed, red-eyed,
rufous-sided angels, in light and shadow, stay half hidden.

THE WILLETS

One stood still, looking stupid. The other,
beak open, streaming a thin sound,
held wings out, took sideways steps,
stamping the salt marsh. It looked threatening.
The other still stood wooden, a decoy.

He stamp-danced closer, his wings arose,
their hinges straightened,
from the wedge-wide beak the thin sound
streaming agony-high—
in fear she wouldn't stand? She stood.

Her back to him pretended—
was it welcome, or only dazed
admission of their fate?
Lifting, he streamed a warning
from his beak, and lit

upon her, trod upon her
back, both careful feet.
The wings held off his weight.
His tail pressed down, slipped off. She
animated. And both went back to fishing.

DR. HENDERSON

Watching Dr. Henderson, who is about eighty,
take his yearly sunbath on the beach:
He unfolds the cretonne-covered lounge
chair, taking approximately 20 minutes
before getting it facing the sun just right,
getting it as level as possible on the
slightly sloping, gravelly sand above the
low-tide line. He sits, is about to lie
down, then interrupts himself to get
the cushion just right under his head,
and the towel just right on the end where
his feet will rest. He has almost lain down,
when he decides to take his loafers off,
and then his black socks. Having pushed
the socks into the shoes in a thorough way,
and placed the shoes neatly beside each other
on the sand to his left, he finds he's hot,
sweating already. So, fumblingly, but
determinedly, he gets off the lounge and
starts to walk to the water.

His feet crimp on the pebbles. It's a slow
process, but finally he feels the water
between his toes, and he stops. He looks
out over the water, the spread of it,
that ripples fairly calmly toward shore:
there is a little breeze, but nothing
dangerous. In his loose, dark blue boxer
shorts, showing a wide flat ass and a high
round belly, sloping shoulders, flaccid arms,
the hands hanging, his pink (but not bald)
scalp shining along the precisely straight
parting of his wavy leghorn-rooster-white
hair, Dr. Henderson sallies into the water.
Slowly. Slowly, and with many hesitations,
he takes a step—or, rather, a shuffle—
with the left foot, then the right, then
pauses, wrists swinging, thumbs and fingers

rubbing together, while he gazes out upon
the small waves—also carefully gazing down
through them—scanning the bottom, making sure
nothing harmful lurks there.

Inch by inch, up the thin shins and sagging
thighs the water rises, cool, then cold,
then a little colder. He shudders, but
presses on, when the water touches and sets
afloat, within the ballooning shorts, his
wrinkled testicles and shrunken dong.
In about 20 minutes he has taken the dozen, or
so, shuffles resulting in the water reaching
his waist. *Then* he lifts his knees! He's
sitting in the water, entirely wet to his chin!
He floats!

Later, having gamely struggled back to shore,
he eventually settles himself on his back
on the lounge. His white head is placed
exactly in the center of the cushion. His
long feet, pronated on callused yellow heels,
are symmetrically set on the folded towel.
Hands, palms down, by the sides of the dripping
dark blue shorts, the shirred bellyband biting
into his thick middle, above which a thin mat
of kinky gray hair flutters in the hot breeze,
pink, big-nosed face, with eyelids and lips firmly
shut, turned up to the sky, Dr. Henderson,
with long-practiced dignity and deliberation,
begins his yearly sunbath on the beach.

THE BEAUTY OF THE HEAD
Shuswap River, Sicamous, B.C.

1

Black bear, pacing the shore, lollops over
a fallen pine. Loon in the swampy inlet lets go
his weird choked cry. Bowl of the lake rocks,
dinghy at the stern champs-stammers. Waves slosh,
my mouth waters, my ear's cochlea fills up,
and empties. I notice how I breathe,
in the cradle of my ribs, to the shift of the lake.
Violet-green swallows slant-fall to a field
of Alpine flowers, where sparse, far-apart blue
wicks, red brushpoints, wink in the moraine.
At night, on the mountain's shoulder pied with
snow, glints the lit hut of a star.
Where we dock this evening, two red-necked
grebe and a loon work their waterlily acre,
dive in turn, and reproject the trumpets
of their necks. Breaking the surface, they break
silence, slip west, silver the last light.
We'll sleep on deck, topside the houseboat,
slap mosquitoes, but first, roast chub
in a flat-stone oven dug on the shore.
These stones, all for skipping, whittled by the lake,
were hot shingles we lay on in sunlight,
drying our hair. Lake is our bathtub, dish-sink,
drinking jug, and (since the boat's head doesn't work,
—the ice box, either—the bilge pump barely)
lake is water closet, too. Little I knew
a gale this night would wash, and then
wind-wipe my rump hung over the rail.

2

Black bear straddles the log he rolled off,
lopes to the lake, wades in a ways, and sips,
lips making a ripple. He lies down like a dog
in the soft silt, then, up with a lurch, he exits.
Bush of the bank closes around his haunches.

Uneasy, I scan the dusky beach. Is he that hole
in the end of a log in the sunset?—that root
of a cottonwood stump?—that near shadow
dilating, indenting the bush?
As wind rises, tide rises. Moon swings out—
anchor that can't catch—and wanders half-circle.
We lie in our sacks, clouds and the mountain
traveling, woods and waves exchanging
horizons, dipping, carousing. We mummy-sacks sway
with the deck. Tied up on a long line to a pine,
the bow starts to strain, stomp, scrape
on shore stones. Aft pushed broadside, the boat is about
to be grounded, while with each ram of rising water,
the dinghy knocks, bucks, whines to mount
the stern. No running lights on the *Alice B.,*
and, its battery weak, the flashlight's beam
has no reach. It's our second mooring.
First night in the river's mouth was calm.
Now, water hard as walls shoves starboard,
wants to fling the boat on a shelf
of ripping, skipping rocks—the first, then the second
shelf—the third would set it next the pines
by morning, low tide leave it really a house
on land. And, in the middle of this
bouncing, howling lake-quake, I have to go.
Backing down the deck ladder is one thing,
perching on the teetering rail (away from portside
where Skipper and Mates are bunked) is another,
hanging on and hanging *out,* in the lurch and clamor—
not minding the dunk, but hoping not to fall
overboard, while going—is toughest of all.
I succeed and, backside baptized, feel
a mariner's talent proved.

3

Three A.M. By four it will be light.
No one nervous but me, the other three asleep.
Bedded down on the bench in the stern,
keeping watch, kept soaked ritualistically
by wave spray, I check the bilge by the dirty

eye of the lamp. Yes, the lake is leaking
to the deck. But, as if mine had pacified it,
big water eases, groans of boat and dinghy
come gradually to cease.
Meaning greater danger? Half the house has climbed
the beach. Unless got under way with the tide high,
here's where we'll stay. So I wake First Mate
and make such a nag it wakes Skipper.
With dawn, the engine started, anchor up, we untie
and, bup-bup-bup, we're off, open throttle
into the wind, over the smacking lake.
Mosquitoes blow off, sun peeps over the mountain.
Wet, ensacked, exhausted I crimp
in the galley-bunk to sleep.

4

My face a knot
became in sleep.
Anxiety and storm.
Confusion.
Not only was my
ground a wave,
but wrestling waves
deformed that wave.
My thoughts were torn,
my hipbones had no rest,
and I was clenched.
Darkness that strangles,
thrashing noise,
the source unknown.
Threat of being smashed
at bottom of a hole—
the cave of a huge,
insane, conglomerating
wave. And sun whipped
my glued eyelids.

Waked, I stood
at the point of the prow,
looking down into clear
water, like a well,
in still mountain shadow.
Anchor twinkled far below
in a slot between
humped stones,
smooth as glass,
where soft-nosed fish
lay moveless, but
for sideways flicks
of their circular eyes.
Boat rocking gently,
tethered to shore.
Brushing my body,
the early wind,
redolent of pine,
freshened and loosened
my forehead.

Tonight we are docked at the top of the lake's
right arm, at a fisherman's inn, awaiting dinner
around a thick oak table. In the window frame,
a crook-treed orchard where a blond horse crops
the flowing grass. A woman, in a wind-torn dress,
brings a full bucket to the buckskin. We play chess
and drink the stinging beer,
while our fish fries in the kitchen.
All secure, on shore for the night, the *Alice B.,*
snugged tight to an iron bust on the pier.
When, squint-eyed from the flashing river,
we climbed into farmyard shade, I spied
the squeaking door of a little privy
of new pine board, among trees beyond
where the blond horse crops. The bright
hook worked like silk. One seat, and no wasps,
it was all mine. An almanac, the pages Bible-thin,
hung by a string through a hole made with an awl.
Outside, steady silence, and in
the slit-moon-window, high up, a fragrant
tassel of pine. Alone, at peace, and journey done,
I sat. Feet planted on dependable planks, I sat.
Engrossed by the beauty of knothole panel before me,
I sat a nice long time.

ABOVE BEAR LAKE

Sky and lake the same blue,
and blue the languid mountain between them.
Cloud fluffs make the scene flow.
Greeny white poles of aspen snake up,
graven with welts and calluses where branches
dried and broke. Other scabs are lover-made:
initials dug within linked hearts and, higher,
some jackknifed peace signs.
A breeze, and the filtered light makes shine
a million bristling quills of spruce and fir
downslope, where slashes of sky and lake
hang blue—windows of intense stain. We take
the rim trail, crushing bloom of sage,
sniffing resinous wind, our boots in the wild,
small, everycolored Rocky Mountain flowers.
Suddenly, a steep drop-off: below we see the whole,
the whale of it—deep, enormous blue—
that widens, while the sky slants back to pale
behind a watercolored mountain.
Western Tanager—we call him "Fireface"—
darts ahead, we climb to our camp
as the sun slips lower. Clipped to the top
of the tallest fir, Olive-Sided Flycatcher,
over and over, fierce-whistles, "Whip!
Whip three bears! Whip, whip three bears!"

THINGS TAKING PLACE

II

NIGHT VISITS WITH THE FAMILY

Sharon's Dream

We were rounding up cattle, riding trees instead of horses.
The way I turned the herd was to let my tree limb grow.
Circling out around an obstinate heifer,
my horse stretched and whipped back, but too slow.

Paul's Dream

Twelve white shirts and I had to iron them.
Some swirled away. They were bundles of cloud.
Hailstones fell and landed as buttons.
I should have picked them up before they melted to mud.

Roy's Dream

Down in the cellar a library of fruit:
berries, pears and apricots published long ago.
Two lids of wax covered my eyelids. A tart title
I couldn't read was pasted on my brow.

Dan's Dream

In the playhouse Dad made when I was six
I put my captive hawk. The chimney had a lid
that locked. The wallpaper was faded and fouled.
I couldn't wake, and dirty feathers filled my little bed.

Grace's Dream

Hindleg in the surf, my grand piano, groaning,
crawled ashore. I saw that most of the black keys
had been extracted, their roots were bleeding. It tried
to embrace me while falling forward on three knees.

Margaret's Dream

There was an earthquake and Jordan's boot got caught
in a crack in the street. His bike had fallen through
and went on peddling underneath, came up the basement
stairs to warn me what had happened. That's how I knew.

Betty's Dream

Aunt Etta was wearing a wig, of wilver. Its perfection
made you see how slack her chins were. Under the hair
in front was a new eye, hazel and laughing. It winked.
"You, too, will be seventy-two," she said. It gave me a scare.

George's Dream

Old Glory rippling on a staff. No, it was a maypole,
and the ribbons turned to rainbows. I saw a cat
climbing the iridescent bow. Then I was sliding down
a banister. My uniform split in the crotch, I was so fat.

Corwin's Dream

With my new camera I was taking a picture of my old
camera. The new one was guaranteed; it was the kind
that issues instant color prints. What came out
was an X-ray of the tunnel in the roller of a window blind.

Ruth's Dream

Standing under the shower I was surprised
to see I wasn't naked. The streams had dressed
me in a gown of seed pearls, and gloves that my nails
poked through like needles. They pricked if I touched my breast.

Steve's Dream

Two tiny harmonicas. I kept them in my mouth,
and sucked them. That made twin secret tunes.
Mother said, "What is it you are always humming?"
I told her they were only the stones of prunes.

Diane's Dream

Grandmother wasn't dead. Only her ring finger.
Before we buried it, we must remove the ruby.
And the finger was jackknifed. I offered to unclench it,
but couldn't do it. I was too much of a booby.

May's Dream

Cowpuncher on a tree-horse wears
a cloud-shirt with hailstone buttons.
He rides and, through wax eyelids, reads
a library of fruit. He passes a hawk
locked in a playhouse, a grand piano
with three broken knees. Nothing he can do
about any of these. When old, an Auntie
in a wilver wig, he goes. He's almost too fat
to slide down the rainbow's banister that
ends in a gray X-ray of a tunnel in the blind.
There he wears a water dress, tastes secret tunes.
Until I wake he cannot die. Until I wake,
the ruby lives on the dead finger.

NATURE

A large gut, this was the vision.
Mother in hospital, I slept in her bed.
Inside a stomach great as the planet . . .

quagmire ground in gray movement . . .
mucous membrane, rugous, reached my foot
. . . sucked one leg to the crotch . . .

Squirming, sweating, I pulled loose this time.
But it surrounds,
shudders, munches, sucks us down, so

gradually we seldom know.
Until the last sink, where mouth says,
"Here's a Mouth!" Is Nature

this planet only? Or all the universe?
What should we think? Birth
of an infant . . . a film I saw the other day:

Mother-belly, round as the planet,
her navel the North Pole . . .
palpated by rubber fingers . . . Face down,

the wet head, twisting free
of a vomiting Mouth, its mouth
tasting anus as, forced forth, it howled . . .

Muck sealed the squeezed eyes . . .
Mother, eighty-one, fasted five days
and went to Temple. Mormon, her creed

eternal life, she fell
on the kitchen floor unconscious.
The plane flew

over snow-breasts of mountains
no man's track has touched.
June, and blue lilacs in every yard . . .

One bud-nippled bloom I took to her hospital bed.
Her mouth woke to its dew. This time
it woke . . . Last night I slept in her bed.

THAT THE SOUL MAY WAX PLUMP

"He who has reached the highest degree of
emptiness will be secure in repose."
—*A Taoist Saying*

My dumpy little mother on the undertaker's slab
had a mannequin's grace. From chin to foot
the sheet outlined her, thin and tall. Her face
uptilted, bloodless, smooth, had a long smile.
Her head rested on a block under her nape,
her neck was long, her hair waved, upswept. But later,
at "the viewing," sunk in the casket in pink tulle,
an expensive present that might spoil, dressed
in Eden's green apron, organdy bonnet on,
she shrank, grew short again, and yellow. Who
put the gold-rimmed glasses on her shut face, who
laid her left hand with the wedding ring on
her stomach that really didn't seem to be there
under the fake lace?

Mother's work before she died was self-purification,
a regimen of near starvation, to be worthy to go
to Our Father, Whom she confused (or, more aptly, fused)
with our father, in Heaven long since. She believed
in evacuation, an often and fierce purgation,
meant to teach the body to be hollow, that the soul
may wax plump. At the moment of her death, the wind
rushed out from all her pipes at once. Throat and rectum
sang together, a galvanic spasm, hiss of ecstasy.
Then, a flat collapse. Legs and arms flung wide,
like that female Spanish saint slung by the ankles
to a cross, her mouth stayed open in a dark O. So,
her vigorous soul whizzed free. On the undertaker's slab, she
lay youthful, cool, triumphant, with a long smile.

BIRTHDAY

What am I doing here?
What are the waves doing running?—
the grass doing growing?
What is the worm doing
making its hole?—
the sun glowing?—the stone
sitting unmoving. Remove
the stone: A shadow is missing.

The moon is making its circle.
A moth is emerging.
A mountain is shifting. A forest
is burning. A snake
is leaving its skin. A fig tree
is bearing. What am I doing here—
the waves running and hissing?

Dawn is doing its breaking.
The grass is growing.
A buttercup fills with light.
What am I doing? What am I making?
What is the stone doing? Making
its shadow. The worm
is making its hole.

RUNNING ON THE SHORE

The sun is hot, the ocean cool. The waves
throw down their snowy heads. I run
under their hiss and boom, mine their wild
breath. Running the ledge where pipers
prod their awls into sand-crab holes,
my barefoot tracks their little prints cross
on wet slate. Circles of romping water swipe
and drag away our evidence. Running and
gone, running and gone, the casts of our feet.

My twin, my sprinting shadow on yellow shag,
wand of summer over my head, it seems
that we could run forever while the strong
waves crash. But sun takes its belly under.
Flashing above magnetic peaks of the ocean's
purple heave, the gannet climbs,
and turning, turns
to a black sword that drops,
hilt-down, to the deep.

SCROPPO'S DOG

In the early morning, past the shut houses,
past the harbor shut in fog, I walk free and
single. It is summer—that's lucky. The whole
day is mine. At the end of our village I stop
to greet Scroppo's dog, whose chain is wrapped
around a large dusty boulder. His black coat
is gray, from crouching every day in the gravel
of Scroppo's yard—a yard by a scrap-filled pond,
where Scroppo deals in wrecked cars and car parts.
I guess he gets them from crashes on the expressway,
or from abandoned junks he loots by the roadside.

I don't know the name of Scroppo's dog. I remember
him, years ago, as a big fierce-looking pup.
It may have been his first day chained there,
or shortly after, that he first greeted me:
his eyes big nuggets shooting orange sparks, his
red tongue rippling out between clean fangs—
fangs as white as lilies of the valley that bloom
in a leafy border by Scroppo's weathered porch.
It was late May, as now, when with sudden joyful
bark, black fur erect and gleaming, the dog
rushed toward me—but was stopped by his chain,
a chain then bright and new. I would have met
and stroked him, but didn't dare get near him,
in his strangled frenzy—in his unbelief—
that something at his throat cut short
his coming, going, leaping, circling, running—
something he couldn't bite through, tripped him:
he could go only so far: to the trash in the weeds
at the end of the driveway, to the edge
of the oily, broken cement in back, where Scroppo's
muddy flatbed truck stands at night.

Now, as I walk toward him, the dog growls,
then cowers back. He is old and fat and dirty,
and his eyes spit equal hate and fear.

He knows exactly how far he can strain
from the rock and the wrapped chain. There's
a trench in a circle in the oily dirt his paws
have dug. Days and weeks and months and years
of summer heat and winter cold have been survived
within the radius of that chain.
Scroppo's dog knows me, and wants to come and
touch. At the same time, his duty to expel
the intruder makes him bare his teeth and
bristle. He pounds his matted tail, he snarls
while cringing, alternately stretches toward me,
and springs back. His bark, husky and cracked,
follows me for a block, until I turn the corner,
crossing the boundary of the cove.

I've never touched Scroppo's dog, and his
yearning tongue has never licked me. Yet, we
know each other well. Subject to the seasons'
extremes, confined to the limits of our yard,
early fettered by an obscure master in whose
power we bask, bones grow frail while steel
thickens; while rock fattens, passions and
senses pale. Scroppo's dog sniffs dust.
He sleeps a lot. My nose grown blunt, I need
to remember the salty damp of the air's taste
on summer mornings, first snowfall's freshness,
the smoke of burning leaves. Each midday,
when the firehouse whistle blows, a duet
of keen, weird howls is heard, as, at the steep
edge of hopelessness, with muzzle pointed,
ears flat, eyes shut, Scroppo's dog forlornly
yodels in time to the village siren sounding noon.

RED MOONSET

Spinnaker

of a tipping ship

the moon low

large. Watermelon

wedge. A clot

of midnight

cloud sucks

sinks it. Bitten

about out. But

one more ripe

inflation. Chinks

in a chunk

of fire.

SEPTEMBER THINGS

Brutal sound of acorns
falling. Chokecherry-ink
beads have dried. On tile

bare feet still feel
stored warmth, eyes graze
a field of blue

water. A few languid
boats like flecks
of paint far out,

the lanyards tinkling.
Snag-nailed surf reaches,
drags back, over echoing

pebbles. A lateborn
cardinal ticks and
whistles—too pale

and thin. Too vivid,
the last pink
petunia's indrawn mouth.

OCTOBER

1

A smudge for the horizon
that, on a clear day, shows
the hard edge of hills and
buildings on the other coast.
Anchored boats all head one way:
north, where the wind comes from.
You can see the storm inflating
out of the west. A dark hole
in gray cloud twirls, widens,
while white rips multiply
on the water far out.
Wet tousled yellow leaves,
thick on the slate terrace.
The jay's hoarse cry. He's
stumbling in the air,
too soaked to fly.

2

Knuckles of the rain
on the roof,
chuckles into the drain-
pipe, spatters on
the leaves that litter
the grass. Melancholy
morning, the tide full
in the bay, an overflowing
bowl. At least, no wind,
no roughness in the sky,
its gray face bedraggled
by its tears.

3

Peeling a pear, I remember
my daddy's hand. His thumb
(the one that got nipped by the saw,
lacked a nail) fit into
the cored hollow of the slippery

half his knife skinned so neatly.
Dad would pare the fruit from our
orchard in the fall, while Mother
boiled the jars, prepared for
"putting up." Dad used to darn
our socks when we were small,
and cut our hair and toenails.
Sunday mornings, in pajamas, we'd
take turns in his lap. He'd help
bathe us sometimes. Dad could do
anything. He built our dining table,
chairs, the buffet, the bay window
seat, my little desk of cherry wood
where I wrote my first poems. That
day at the shop, splitting panel
boards on the electric saw (oh, I
can hear the screech of it now,
the whirling blade that sliced
my daddy's thumb) he received the mar
that, long after, in his coffin,
distinguished his skilled hand.

4

I sit with braided fingers
and closed eyes
in a span of late sunlight.
The spokes are closing.
It is fall: warm milk of light,
though from an aging breast.
I do not mean to pray.
The posture for thanks or
supplication is the same
as for weariness or relief.
But I am glad for the luck
of light. Surely it is godly,
that it makes all things
begin, and appear, and become
actual to each other.
Light that's sucked into
the eye, warming the brain
with wires of color.

Light that hatched life
out of the cold egg of earth.

5

Dark wild honey, the lion's
eye color, you brought home
from a country store.
Tastes of the work of shaggy
bees on strong weeds,
their midsummer bloom.
My brain's electric circuit
glows, like the lion's iris
that, concentrated, vibrates
while seeming not to move.
Thick transparent amber
you brought home,
the sweet that burns.

6

"The very hairs of your head
are numbered," said the words
in my head, as the haircutter
snipped and cut, my round head
a newel poked out of the tent
top's slippery sheet, while my
hairs' straight rays rained
down, making pattern on the neat
vacant cosmos of my lap. And
maybe it was those tiny flies,
phantoms of my aging eyes, seen
out of the sides floating (that,
when you turn to find them
full face, always dissolve) but
I saw, I think, minuscule,
marked in clearest ink, Hairs
#9001 and #9002 fall, the cut-off
ends streaking little comets,
till they tumbled to confuse
with all the others in their
fizzled heaps, in canyons of my
lap. And what keeps asking

in my head now that, brushed off
and finished, I'm walking
in the street, is how can those
numbers remain all the way through,
and all along the length of every
hair, and even before each one
is grown, apparently, through
my scalp? For, if the hairs of my
head are numbered, it means
no more and no less of them
have ever, or will ever be.
In my head, now cool and light,
thoughts, phantom white flies,
take a fling: This discovery
can apply to everything.

7

Now and then, a red leaf riding
the slow flow of gray water.
From the bridge, see far into
the woods, now that limbs are bare,
ground thick-littered. See,
along the scarcely gliding stream,
the blanched, diminished, ragged
swamp and woods the sun still
spills into. Stand still, stare
hard into bramble and tangle,
past leaning broken trunks,
sprawled roots exposed. Will
something move?—some vision
come to outline? Yes, there—
deep in—a dark bird hangs
in the thicket, stretches a wing.
Reversing his perch, he says one
"Chuck." His shoulder-patch
that should be red looks gray.
This old redwing has decided to
stay, this year, not join the
strenuous migration. Better here,
in the familiar, to fade.

ON ITS WAY

Orange on its way to ash.
Anger that a night will quench.
Passion in its honey swell
pumpkin-plump before the rot.
Bush of fire everywhere.
Fur of hillside running flame.
Rush of heat to rosehip cheek.
Ripeness on its way to frost.
Glare of blood before the black.
Foxquick pulse. The sun a den.
Heartkill. And the gold a gun.
It is death that tints the leaves.

NOVEMBER NIGHT

Sky's face so old,
one eyeball loose,

fallen to the side,
the walleyed moon,

among the mouse-gray
waves, its squints

of mercury roll.
An aging face slips

its symmetry; lip
lags, lid droops.

Behind the horizon
the slide begins,

of a blind,
thick-furred tide:

rat-swells rip
and top each other,

gulp each other,
bloat, and scoot

pale vomit out
on a moonless shore.

THIS MORNING

My glasses are
dirty. The window
is dirty. The binocs
don't focus exactly.
Outside it's about
to snow. Not to mention
my myopia, my migraine
this morning, mist on
the mirror, my age.
Oh, there is the cardinal,
color of apple I used to
eat off my daddy's tree.
Tangy and cocky, he
drops to find
a sunflower seed in
the snow. New snow
is falling on top
of the dirty snow.

VIEW TO THE NORTH

As you grow older, it gets colder.
You see through things.
I'm looking through the trees,

their torn and thinning leaves,
to where chill blue water
is roughened by wind.

Day by day the scene opens,
enlarges, rips of space
appear where full branches

used to snug the view.
Soon it will be wide, stripped,
entirely unobstructed:

I'll see right through
the twining waves, to
the white horizon, to the place

where the North begins.
Magnificent! I'll be thinking
while my eyeballs freeze.

THE THICKENING MAT

My track the first
on new snow:
each step, with soft
snap, pressed
a padded button
into a thickening
mat—snug sensation,
satisfying pattern—
to the corner,
where I turned and

met the wind:
whips to my eyes
and mouth. This way
all I breathe
is snow. Marks
of my feet, unique,
black-edged under
the streetlight—
where are they?
All blank, all white.

COLD COLORS

Sweetpea

pinks

in the winter.

Sun sets

through thin

windy

branches

dark

like snarled string

over water's hard

stretched white scratched

skin.

On sky's

clear royal icy

cheek blush

tints

of spring.

CAPTAIN HOLM

I see Captain Holm
in yellow slicker,
right hand behind him
on the stick of the tiller,
feet in the well
of his orange Sailfish:
like a butterfly's
single wing, it slants
upright over the bay.
Captain Holm, our neighbor,
eighty years old,
thin and sclerotic,
can still fold
legs into the hull,
balance a bony buttock
on the shelf of the stern.
With a tug at the mainstay
he makes his sail trim up,
sniffs out whatever wind there is.
This raw day,
Captain Holm's alone,
his scrap of color
the only one
on the wide bay.
Winter sunset transfuses
that frail wing.

DIGGING IN THE GARDEN OF AGE I UNCOVER A LIVE ROOT
(For E.W.)

The smell of wet geraniums. On furry
leaves, transparent drops rounded
as cats' eyes seen sideways.
Smell of the dark earth, and damp
brick of the pots you held, tamped empty.
Flash of the new trowel. Your eyes
green in greenhouse light. Smell of
your cotton smock, of your neck
in the freckled shade of your hair.
A gleam of sweat in your lip's scoop.
Pungent geranium leaves, their wet
smell when our widening pupils met.

TODAY

Beneath the tongue a stem of mercury rises.
A needle flicks in orbit on the ticking wrist.
At 6 A.M. an earthquake in Los Angeles.
The finger dials. Dainty electronic dots
imprint a distant micromandala on the mind.
Sunny and 90 there, everything shaking. Here,
on Long Island, calmly snowing at 9. Inside its
wrap, our planet swirls, one minute makes 60
separate leaps, graphs decode the finite waves,
tally the roots of grass. Outside the amnion,
what time is it?—what heat, what equilibrium,
what weight? Three human probes from moon
drop home today. In a frame of constant
jerky light, a trinket of metal, friction-scorched,
is scooped from sea. Technical inputs for this
report: Key touch total = 762. Temperature =
99.1 F. Sound-wave length = 3000 miles.

SURVEY OF THE WHOLE

World's lopsided
                    That's its trouble
Don't run in a circle
                    Runs in a loop
        Too much winter
                    In the wrong place
        Too much summer
                    Around the sun
        World's gimpy
                    Been turning so long
            It's lumpy
                    A bad top
Day's not long enough
                    Spins on a nail
        Night's too long
                    Bent out of kilter
        World's a lemon
                    Wobbles in a loop
        Around the sun
                    It's not an orange
Won't ever be sweet
                    Turns too fast
        Turns too slow
                    Can't ripen
        Too much desert
                    Too much snow

THE SOLAR CORONA*

Looks like a large
pizza with too much
tomato sauce (the fiery

islands in the melted
cheese, the jagged rim,
red bulge of crust)

served on a square
black tray, a "spectro
heliographic diagram

of the sun in the extreme
ultraviolet region of
the spectrum." This

pizza is 400 times
larger than the moon.
Don't burn your lips!—

the deep red regions
are coolest, the white
(ricotta) hottest.

*Cover picture on the *Scientific American,* October 1973

FIRST WALK ON THE MOON

Ahead, the sun's face in a flaring hood,
was wearing the moon, a mask of shadow
that stood between. Cloudy earth
waned, gibbous, while our target grew:
an occult bloom, until it lay beneath
the fabricated insect we flew. Pitched
out of orbit we yawed in, to impact
softly on that circle.

               Not "ground"
the footpads found for traction.
So far, we haven't the name.
So call it "terrain," pitted and pocked
to the round horizon (which looked
too near): a slope of rubble where
protuberant cones, dish-shaped hollows,
great sockets glared, half blind
with shadow, and smaller sucked-in folds
squinted, like blowholes on a scape
of whales.

             Rigid and pneumatic, we
emerged, white twin uniforms on the dark
"mare," our heads transparent spheres,
the outer visors gold. The light was
glacier bright, our shadows long,
thin fissures, of "ink." We felt neither
hot nor cold.

             Our boot cleats sank
into "grit, something like glass,"
but sticky. Our tracks remain
on what was virgin "soil." But that's
not the name.

There was no air there,
no motion, no sound outside our heads.
We brought what we breathed
on our backs: the square papooses we
carried were our life sacks. We spoke
in numbers, fed the rat-a-tat-tat of data
to amplified earth. We saw no spoor
that any had stepped before us. Not
a thing has been born here, and nothing
has died, we thought.

We had practiced
to walk, but we toddled (with caution,
lest ambition make us fall
to our knees on that alien "floor").
We touched nothing with bare hands.
Our gauntlets lugged the cases of gear,
deployed our probes and emblems,
set them prudently near the insect liftoff
station, with its flimsy ladder to home.

All day it was night, the sky black
vacuum, though the strobe of the low sun
smote ferocious on that "loam."
We could not stoop, but scooped up
"clods" of the clinging "dust," that flowed
and glinted black, like "graphite."
So, floating while trotting, hoping not
to stub our toe, we chose and catalogued
unearthly "rocks." These we stowed.

And all night it was day, you could say,
with cloud-cuddled earth in the zenith,
a ghost moon that swiveled. The stars
were all displaced, or else were not
the ones we knew. Maneuvering by numbers
copied from head to head, we surveyed
our vacant outpost. Was it a "petrified
sea bed," inert "volcanic desert," or
crust over quivering "magma," that might
quake?

It was possible to stand there.
And we planted a cloth "flower":
our country colors we rigged to blow
in the non-wind. We could not lift
our arms eye-high (they might deflate)
but our camera was a pistol, the trigger
built into the grip, and we took each
other's pictures, shooting from the hip.
Then bounced and loped euphoric,
enjoying our small weight.

Our flash
eclipsed the sun at takeoff. We left our
insect belly "grounded," and levitated,
standing in its head. The dark dents
of our boots, unable to erode, mark how
we came: two white mechanic knights,
the first, to make tracks in some kind
of "sand." The footpads found it solid, so
we "landed." But that's not the right name.

Note: The men of Apollo 11, arriving in their landing module, *Eagle,* were the first to
put tracks on the moon, 1969.

"SO LONG" TO THE MOON
FROM THE MEN OF APOLLO

A nipple, our parachute
covers the capsule: an
aureole, on a darker aureole

like the convex spiral of
a mollusk, on a great breast:
the skin removed: agitated

glandular pattern revealed:
the SPLASH, seen from above,
from the helicopter:

Apollo 17 comes home
to the Pacific: the moon
strewn with our trash:

module platforms, crashed LMs,
metal flags and plaques, dead
sensor devices like inside-out

umbrellas, a golf ball. A small
steel alloy astronaut doll
bites the black dust.

THE PURE SUIT OF HAPPINESS

The pure suit of happiness,
not yet invented. How I long
to climb into its legs,

fit into its sleeves, and zip
it up, pull the hood
over my head. It's got

a face mask, too, and gloves
and boots attached. It's
made for me. It's blue. It's

not too heavy, not too
light. It's my right.
It has its own weather,

which is youth's breeze,
equilibrated by the ideal
thermostat of maturity,

and built in, to begin with,
fluoroscopic goggles of
age. I'd see through

everything, yet be happy.
I'd be suited for life. I'd
always look good to myself.

TELEOLOGY

The eyes look front in humans.
Horse or dog could not shoot,

seeing two sides to everything.
Fish, who never shut their eyes,

can swim on their sides, and see
two worlds: blunt dark below;

above, the daggering light.
Round as a burr, the eye

its whole head, the housefly
sees in a whizzing circle.

Human double-barreled eyes,
in their narrow blind trained

forward, hope to shoot and hit
—if they can find it—

the backward-speeding hole
in the Cyclops face of the future.

TEETH

Teeth are so touchy. They're part of your skeleton.
Laid out on the dentist's couch, you're being strummed.
Still vibrant. For how long? You're shown an X-ray

of the future: how the lower jaw has wandered away
into a neighbor's lot. The fillings glitter,
but it's glowworm's work by now.

A skull white as enamel,
the fontanelle's fine stitchery can be admired.
Does it remember being covered

with scraggly hair, like a coconut?
Bald as a baby, and with one wide bucktooth left,
you have the upturned grin of a carefree clown.

So you drool and spit out. That's only
temporary. There'll be just one big cavity soon.
You'll be dry—yes, dry as a bone.

DEATHS

One will die   in a low little house in the snow.
One will die   on the mountain.
One will die   at a table. Red will spread on the white cloth.
One will die   on a trolley, will fall from the platform,
                rounding a curve. Soon after, the trolley will die.
One will die   in the bathtub. Slippery, heavy to remove. . . . Not die
                from cut veins or flooded lungs. From embolism
                at the end of the birthday party. The angel cake
                will hold 61 candles. . . . How do I know
                the number of the candles?
One will die   in a celebrated bed, where his grandfather died,
                where his father died, where his son will die.
One will die   in her wheelchair. She has lived there 50 years.
One will die   on a porch, on a summer day.
One will die   on the stairs of the same house, the same day, and
                robbers, with their gags and knives, will get clean away.
One will die   not knowing she dies, for three years suckled by
                machine, emptied by machine, made to tick and breathe
                by machine. Without moving, without speaking,
                she will grant 1000 interviews.
One will die   in the death of a plane, one in the death of a ship,
                another under a stumbling horse that breaks its neck.
One will die   in the hall outside his locked door, having forgotten
                the key inside.
One will die   made to die by one enraged, who will beg to die
                "like a man" by bullet instead of the hell
                of a lifetime in a cell. He will die a lifetime
                in a cell.
One will die   while driving a hearse. The coffin, spilled
                on the highway, will detour the traffic in which
                a cab containing one about to give birth will die.
One will die   about to be born.
One will die   in hospital, having gone to visit his friend, who,
                in eternal pain, has prayed to die, and envies
                that unexpected end. He, too, will die.
All will die   in the end.

THE WONDERFUL PEN

I invented a wonderful pen. Not a typewriter . . . I wanted to use
just one hand, the right. With my hand always bent, the ink tube
a vein in my wrist, fixed between finger and thumb the pen wrote
as fast as I could feel. It chose all the right words for my feelings.
But then, my feelings ran out through the pen. It went dry. I had
a book of wonderful feelings, but my right hand was paralyzed.
I threw away the pen.

I invented a dream camera: a box, with a visor or mask . . . like a
stereopticon. When I awoke, I could view, and review, my dreams,
entire, in their depth. Events, visions, symbols, colors without
names, dazzled, obsessed me. They scalded my sight. I threw
away the camera. I had a moving picture of my wonderful dreams,
but I was blind.

So, with my left hand I wrote. I had been lazy so long . . .
The letters went backwards across the page. Sometimes they went
upside down: a "q" for a "b," a "d" for a "p," or an "n" for a "u,"
an "m" for a "w." And it got worse. Now, since I can't read, or
see, not even the mirror can tell me, what I mean by the first
line by the time I've written the last line. But my feelings
are back, and my dreams . . .

What I write is so hard to write. It must be hard to read.
So slow . . . So swift my mind, so stupid my pen. I think I'll invent
a typewriter . . . For the left hand, and no eyes. No! I throw
away the thought. But I have a wonderful mind: Inventive. It is
for you to find. Read *me.* Read my mind.

ENDING

Maybe there *is* a Me inside of me
and, when I lie dying, he
will crawl out. Through my toe.
Green on the green rug, and then
white on the wall, and then
over the windowsill, up the trunk
of the apple tree, he
will turn brown and rough and warty
to match the bark. But you'll be
able to see —(*who* will be
able to see?) his little jelly
belly pulsing with the heart inside
his transparent hide.
And, once on the top bough,
tail clinging, as well as "hands,"
he'll turn the purest blue
against the sky—
(say it's a clear day, and I don't die
at night). Maybe from there
he'll take wing—That's it!—
an ARCHAEOPTERYX! Endless,
the possibilities, my little Soul,
once you exit from my toe.
But, oh,
looking it up, I read:
"Archaeopteryx, generally considered
the first bird . . . [although]
closely related to certain small
dinosaurs . . . could not fly."
A pain . . . Oh, I
feel a pain in my toe!

DREAM AFTER NANOOK

Lived savage and simple, where teeth were tools.

Killed the caught fish, cracked his back in my jaws.
Harpooned the heavy seal, ate his steaming liver raw.
Wore walrus skin for boots and trousers. Made knives
    of tusks. Carved the cow-seal out of her hide
    with the horn of her husband.

Lived with huskies, thick-furred as they.
Snarled with them over the same meat.
Paddled a kayak of skin, scooted sitting over the water.
Drove a skein of dogs over wide flats of snow.
Tore through the tearing wind with my whip.

Built a hive of snow-cubes cut from the white ground.
Set a square of ice for window in the top.
Slid belly-down through the humped doorhole.
Slept naked in skins by the oily thighs
    of wife and pup-curled children.

Rose when the ice-block lightened, tugged the chewed boots on.

Lived in a world of fur—fur ground—jags of ivory.
Lived blizzard-surrounded as a husky's ruff.
Left game-traps under the glass teeth of ice.
Snared slick fish. Tasted their icy blood.
Made a sled with runners of leather.

Made a hat from the armpit of a bear.

SELECTED POEMS

from Iconographs

THE
SUNBIRD
SETTLES
TO ITS
NEST

Boys are swimming through the sun's tail,
which is switched by abrasive waves dyed
flamingo. The head of the sun is cardinal

from the ears down. Its pate is pink. Oh,
as I wrote that, a flush spread to the
hairline. The chin's no longer there.

The tail on the waves is sliced with purple.
Oiled ibis-feathered swells make it fan
out like a peacock's. Then, slowly

dropped and narrowed, it drags west.
The boys' heads are hubs for scintillating
circles. Their arms plough a waterfield

of eyes. The peckered scalp is melting—
there goes the last capfeather, of faint
red down down. Down. The boys come up

almost black. They flip wet off
by the green-haired rocks,
behind them, embered, a phoenix crown.

ROCKY POINT

The mainland looks much smaller than the island,
and faint, implying thinner paint
brushed in as background,
so not as real.
        Here is the present; over there, the past.
        Hard to feel how it's the larger body, that dream-haze,
blue and green wave of land,
not clear, nor seeming solid, as the water in between
it and the rocky point I stand on,
that's lifesized, well detailed with sunlit trees.

        The island looks much bigger than the mainland.
        This shore is foreground. Why have a figure
with its back turned, focused on a streak in the distance,
a coast it can't make out—
that even the sun forgets on foggy days?
        That *is* the larger body, that's a fact—
and would be again, if I were over there. Packed
with central life, it's the torso; this, at best, a leg.
No, a toe. Well, even that is inexact.

        If I think of the whole body, what was vast
in retrospect—now small, thin in the blue of forget—
was, is, but a hand's breadth. *And*
an island. All that's earth is,
on the world's whirled wavedrop.
        And this now present outcrop
that a magnified wave grapples, every fingernail of foam
real to my thirsty eye—
I on a cliff *before* the foreground—
the brush can't paint itself, is but a hair—
oh, it is mainland, it's the moment's ground I stand on,
it is fair.

BEGINNING TO SQUALL

A Buoy like a man in a red sou'wester
is uP to the toP of its Boots in the water
    leaning to warn a Blue Boat

        that, BoBBing and shrugging, is nodding "No,"
            till a strong wave comes and it shivers "Yes."
                The white and the green Boats are quiBBling, too.
                    What is it they don't want to do?

The Bay goes on Bouncing anchor floats,
their colors tennis and tangerine.
Two ruffled gulls laughing are laughing gulls,
    a finial Pair on the gray Pilings.

        Now the Boats are Buttoning slickers on
            which resemBle little tents.
                The Buoy is jumPing uP and down
                    showing a Black Belt stenciled "1."

A yellow Boat's last to lower sail
to wraP like a Bandage around the Boom.
    Blades are sharPening in the water
        that Brightens while the sky goes duller.

A SUBJECT OF THE WAVES

Today, while a steamshovel rooted in the cove,
leveling a parking lot for the new nightclub,
and a plane drilled between clean clouds in the October sky,
and the flags on the yachts tied in the basin flipped in the wind,
I watched my footsteps mark the sand by the tideline.
Some hollow horseshoe crab shells scuttled there,
given motion by the waves. I threw a plank back to the waves
that they'd thrown up, a sun-dried, sea-swollen stave
from a broken dinghy, one end square, one pointed, painted green.
Watching its float, my attention snagged and could not get off
the hook of its experience. I had launched a subject
of the waves I could not leave until completed.

Easily it skipped, putting out, prow-end topping every smack
and swell. It kept its surface dry, and looked to float
beyond the jetty head, and so be loose,
exchange the stasis of the beach
for unconceived fluidities and agitations.
It set sail by the luck of its construction.
Lighter than the forceful waves, it surmounted their shove.
Heavier, steadier than the hollows they scooped behind them,
it used their crested threats for coasting free.
Unsplashed by even a drop of spray, it was casual master
of the inconsistent element it rode.

But there was a bias to the moving sea.
The growth and motion of each wave looked arbitrary,
but the total spread (of which each crease was part,
the outward hem lying flat by the wall of sky
at the dim blue other end of the bay's bed)
was being flung, it seemed, by some distant will.
Though devious and shifty in detail, the whole expanse
reiterated constancy and purpose.
So, just as the arrowy end of the plank, on a peak of a wave,
made a confident leap that would clear the final shoal,
a little sideways breaker nudged it enough
to turn it broadside. Then a swifter slap from a stronger comber
brought it back, erasing yards of its piecemeal progress
with one push. Yet the plank turned point to the tide,

and tried again — though not as buoyant, for it had got soaked.
Arrogance undamaged, it conveyed itself again
over obstacle waves, a courageous ski,
not noticing, since turned from shore, that the swells it conquered
slid in at a slant; that while it met them head on,
it was borne closer to shore, and shunted down the coast.

Now a bulge, a series of them, as a pulse quickened in the tide,
without resistance lifted up the plank, flipped it over twice,
and dumped it in the shallows. It scraped on sand.
And so it was put back. Not at the place of its first effort;
a greater disgrace than that: at before the birth
of balance, pride, intention, enterprise.
It changed its goal, and I changed my ambition. Not the open
sea — escape into rough and wild, into unpredictability —
but rescue, return and rest. Release from influence
became my hope for the green painted, broken slat,
once part of a boat.

Its trials to come ashore the cold will of the waves thwarted
more capriciously than its assays into adventure made before.
Each chance it took to dig, with its bent spike,
a grip in the salvage of pebbles and weed and shell
was teasingly, tirelessly outwitted
by dragouts and dousings, slammings and tuggings
of the punishing sea. Until, of its own impulse, the sea
decided to let be,
and lifted and laid, lifted and laid
the plank inert on sand. At tide turn,
such the unalterable compulsion of the sea,
it had to turn its back and rumple its bed
toward the other edge, the farther side of the spread.

I watched my footsteps mark the sand by the tideline.
The steamshovel rooting in the cove had leveled
a parking lot for the new nightclub.
The launch from the yacht basin whooshed around the end
of the pier, toward a sailboat with dropped anchor there,
whose claxon and flipping flag signaled for pickup.
The men with their mallets had finished sinking posts
by the gangplank entrance to the old ferry,

its hold ballasted with cement, painted green and black,
furnished with paneled bar and dining deck.
I watched them hang a varnished sign between the posts,
and letter the name: *The Ark*.
Tomorrow I must come
out again into the sun,
and mark the sand, and find my plank,
for its destiny's not done.

STONE GULLETS

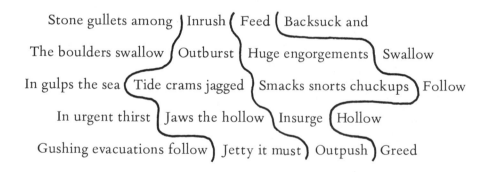

Stone gullets among) Inrush (Feed (Backsuck and

The boulders swallow ∫ Outburst (Huge engorgements (Swallow

In gulps the sea (Tide crams jagged) Smacks snorts chuckups) Follow

In urgent thirst (Jaws the hollow \ Insurge (Hollow

Gushing evacuations follow) Jetty it must) Outpush) Greed

GEOMETRID

Writhes, rides down
on his own spit,
lets breeze twist

him so he chins,
humps, reels up it,
munching back

the vomit string.
Some drools
round his neck.

Arched into a staple
now, high on green
oak leaf he punctures

for food, what
was the point
of his act? Not

to spangle the air,
or show me his trick.
Breeze broke

his suck,
so he spit
a fraction of self's

length forth, bled
colorless from within,
to catch a balance,

glide to a knot
made with his own mouth.
Ruminant

while climbing, got
back better than bitten
leaf. Breeze

that threw
him snagged him
to a new.

THE DNA MOLECULE

The DNA Molecule is The Nude Descending a Staircase,
a circular one. See the undersurfaces of the spiral
treads and the spaces in between. She is descending
and, at the same time, ascending, and she moves
around herself. For she is the staircase, "a proto-
plasmic framework that twists and turns." She is a
double helix, mounting and dismounting around the
swivel of her imaginary spine.

The Nude named DNA can be constructed as a model with
matches and a ribbon of tape. Be sure to use only
four colors on two white strands of twistable tape.
"Only matches of complementary colors may be placed
opposite each other. The pairs are to be Red and Green,
and Yellow and Blue." Make your model as high as the
Empire State Building, and you have an acceptable
replica of The Nude. But (and this is harder) you
must make her move in a continuous coil, an alpha helix,
a double spiral downward and upward at once, and you
must make her increase while, at the same time, occupy-
ing the same field. She must be made to maintain
"a basic topography," changing, yet remaining stable,
if she is to perform her function, which is to produce
and reproduce the microsphere.

Such a sphere is invisible to, but omnipresent in, the
naked eye of The Nude. It contains a "central region
and an outer membrane," making it both able to divide
and to make exact copies of itself without limit.
The Nude "has the capacity for replication and trans-
cription" of all genesis. She ingests and regurgitates
the genetic material, it being the material of her own
cell-self. From single she becomes double, and from
double single. As a woman ingests the demon sperm and,

with the same membrane, regurgitates the mitotic double
of herself upon the slide of time, so The DNA Molecule
produces, with a little pop, at the waistline of its
viscous drop, a new microsphere the same size as herself,
which proceeds singly to grow in order to divide and
double itself. So, from single to double and double to
single, and mounting while descending, she expands
while contracts, she proliferates while disappearing,
at both of her ends.

Remember that Red can only be opposite Green, and Blue
opposite Yellow. Remember that the complementary pairs
of matches must differ slightly in length, "for nature's
pairs can be made only with units whose structures
permit an interplay of forces between the partners."

I fixed a Blue match opposite a Red match of the same
length, pointed away from the center on the double strand
of tape. I saw laid a number of eggs on eggs on the
sticky side of a twig. I saw a worm with many feet
grow out of an egg. The worm climbed the twig, a single
helix, and gobbled the magnified edge of a leaf in quick
enormous bites. It then secreted out of itself a gray
floss with which it wrapped itself, tail first, and
so on, until it had completely muffled and encased
itself, head too, as in a mummy sack.

I saw plushy, iridescent wings push moistly out of the
pouch. At first glued together, they began to part.
On each wing I saw a large blue eye, open forever
in the expression of resurrection. The new Nude
released the flanges of her wings, stretching herself
to touch at all points the outermost rim of the
noösphere. I saw that, for her body, from which the
wings expanded, she had retained the worm.

ORBITER 5 SHOWS
HOW EARTH LOOKS FROM THE MOON

There's a woman in the earth, sitting on
her heels. You see her from the back, in three-
quarter profile. She has a flowing pigtail. She's
holding something
in her right hand—some holy jug. Her left arm is thinner,
in a gesture like a dancer. She's the Indian Ocean. Asia is
light swirling up out of her vessel. Her pigtail points to Europe
and her dancer's arm is the Suez Canal. She is a woman
in a square kimono,
bare feet tucked beneath the tip of Africa. Her tail of long hair is
the Arabian Peninsula.

A woman in the earth.

A man in the moon.

Note: The first telephoto of the whole earth, taken from above the moon by Lunar Orbiter 5, was printed in the *New York Times,* August 14, 1967. Poem title is the headline over the photo.

EARTH WILL NOT LET GO

Earth will not let go our foot
except in her sea cup she lets us float.

Thistle seed, first parachute,
and dragonfly, the glider, use wind for skate.
So does flying squirrel, and helicopter
hummingbird, and winged lizard.

But wind is earth's streamered wake where she whirls,
where pterodactyl in leather suit,
and soaring albatross, white yacht, proved
not grace nor corpulence to extremes brought
breaks the sac earth wraps her creatures in, marsupial.

"Only mammal capable of true flight, the bat,"
equipped with sensory parts (modern instrument craft)
swoops blind of blue, unconscious, a closet his orbit,
or a cave; construes by echo, which is radio.
For Icarus is not yet.

The Wright Aeroplane of 1903 was nothing but a big
box kite "in which the pilot lay prone, head forward,
his left hand operating the lever, his hips
in a saddle. Shifting the hips sideways pulled wires
by which the wing tips were warped and the rudder
turned . . . a double action from one movement
controlling balance and direction."

Blue pilot cap cocked like kingfisher's beak,
and heavy round-toed shoes, how droll, he wore.
Belly-down, on the floor of the long, frail, open box,
he steered with his hips' wiggle. Not merely
the magic carpet, but the whole room he took with him,
trusting loops and fickle twists of air.

Lindbergh sat in a wicker chair
in the Cabin of the Spirit, and solo-crossed

the Atlantic in 1927. ". . . Impossible to photograph
the cabin in one view, the actual distance
from back of the seat to face of instrument board
being only thirty-two inches . . . His feet rested
on the rudder control pedals under the instrument
panel. To see ahead, he either used the periscope or
steered to one side while looking out the window."

Enclosed in a sort of kayak, in wicker to save
weight, the single wing his roof, head bonneted and
goggled, like a plucky scaup with swiveled neck
he swam on swells of ocean wind.

Not unencumbered ever, or by muscle and buoyancy
alone, may we climb loose out of earth's rings,
her atmospheres, ionospheres, pastures to our lungs.

Rejecting wings, props, wheels for landing, all bird
and insect things, John Glenn, snug in the tip
of a cartridge, was discharged in 1962; like a spore
within its pod, was launched by blowgun of pure
energy. His lungfood he took with him. His suit
an embryonic sac, the capsule hugged him uterus-tight.

So, tumbling backwards by propulsion, he tore
the planet's web to the edge. But a last elastic
caught him, kept him to its circle. Implosion,
inbuilt, homeward sucked him back, to splashdown
in her sea cup, that salty womb that spewed
the stillborn moon.

To that rock Apollo astronauts would reach,
they must take the earthpouch simulated. And it
may not breach. For earth will not let go our foot,
though headfirst to be born in angel space we make wings,
jets, rockets, orbit tables, spider landing legs.

SEEING JUPITER

A chair was placed
upon the lawn.
In cloak of wind
and shadow, I
sat and bent
my eye upon
a rim of dark
that glittered up
to open heaven.
In the cup
a worn dime,
size of an iris
of anyone's eye:
flat, cold, lost,
found coin
of enormous time.
Some small change
around it: three
little bits swirled,
or else my ragged eye
with wind swung.
In a black
pocket, behind
that blank, hung
hidden a fourth
moon dot; smarting
beneath my tongue,
dreg of ancient mint;
my retina tasted
light how long
dead? My hair
thrashed. Enlarged
upon the lawn,
my chair
I sat in, that wind
and shadow bent,
had slid an inch
toward dawn.

I LOOK AT MY HAND

I look at my hand and see
        it is also his and hers;
the pads of the fingers his,

                the wrists and knuckles hers.
                In the mirror my pugnacious eye
                and ear of an elf, his;

                        my tamer mouth and slant
                                cheekbones hers.
                His impulses my senses swarm,
        her hesitations they gather.
                Father and Mother
                who dropped me,

                an acorn in the wood,
                repository of your shapes
        and inner streams and circles,

                you who lengthen toward heaven,
            forgive me
                that I do not throw

        the replacing green
        trunk when you are ash.
        When you are ash, no
    features shall there be,
tangled of you,
    interlacing hands and faces

            through me
        who hide, still hard,
            far down under your shades—

                        and break my root, and prune my buds,
                                that what can make no replica
                    may spring from me.

FEEL ME

"Feel me to do right, " our father said on his deathbed.
We did not quite know—in fact, not at all—what he meant.
His last whisper was spent as through a slot in a wall.
He left us a key, but how did it fit? "Feel me
to do right." Did it mean that, though he died, he would be felt
through some aperture, or by some unseen instrument
our dad just then had come to know? So, to do right always,
we need but feel his spirit? Or was it merely his apology
for dying? "Feel that I do right in not trying,
as you insist, to stay on your side. There is the wide
gateway and the splendid tower, and you implore me
to wait here, with the worms!"

Had he defined his terms, and could we discriminate
among his motives, we might have found out how to "do right"
before *we* died—supposing he felt he suddenly knew
what dying was. "You do wrong because you do not feel
as I do now," was maybe the sense. "Feel me, and emulate
my state, for I am becoming less dense—I am feeling right
for the first time." And then the vessel burst,
and we were kneeling around an emptiness.

We cannot feel our father now. His power courses through us,
yes, but *he*—the chest and cheek, the foot and palm,
the mouth of oracle—is calm. And we still seek
his meaning. "Feel me," he said, and emphasized that word.
Should we have heard it as a plea for a caress—
a constant caress, since flesh to flesh was all that we
could do right if we would bless him?
The dying must feel the pressure of that question—
lying flat, turning cold from brow to heel—the hot
cowards there above protesting their love, and saying,
"What can we do? Are you all right?" While the wall opens
and the blue night pours through. "What can we do?
We want to do what's right."

"Lie down with me, and hold me, tight. Touch me. Be
with me. Feel with me. *Feel* me to do right."

THE SHAPE OF DEATH

What does love look like?
Death is a cloud, immense
lid is lifted from the
clap of sound.   A white
jaw of fright.   A
white to gray, like a
and burns—then turns
away, filling the whole
Thickly it wraps, between
moon, the earth's green
cocoon, its choking
of death.   Death is a

We know the shape of death.
and awesome.   At first a
eye of light.   There is a
blossom belches from the
pillared cloud churns from
monstrous brain that bursts
sickly black, spilling
sky with ashes of dread.
the clean seas and the
head.   Trapped in its
breath, we know the shape
cloud. What does love look

like?   Is it a particle,
beyond the microscope and
the length of hope?   Is
that we shall never dare
color, and its alchemy?
can it be dug?   Or
it be bought?   Can it be
a shy beast to be caught?
a clap of sound.   Love is
nests within each cell,
is a ray, a seed, a note,
our air and blood.   It is
our very skin, a sheath

a star, invisible entirely,
Palomar?   A dimension past
it a climate far and fair,
discover?   What is its
Is it a jewel in the earth,
dredged from the sea?   Can
sown and harvested?   Is it
Death is a cloud—immense
little and not loud.   It
and it cannot be split.   It
a word, a secret motion of
not alien—it is near—
to keep us pure of fear.

```
                              F
                              I
                              R
                              E
                         I S L A N D

                       The Milky Way
                     above, the milky
                    waves beside,
                  when the sand is night
                 the sea is galaxy.
                The unseparate stars
              mark a twining coast
            with phosphorescent
         surf
       in the black sky's trough.
     Perhaps we walk on black
    star ash, and watch
  the milks of light foam forward, swish and spill
    while other watchers, out
      walking in their white
        great
            swerve,
              gather
            our
                low
                  spark,
                    our little Way
                      the dark
                        glitter
                        in
                          their
                          s
                           i
                            g
                             h
                              t
                               .
```

THE LOWERING*

The flag is folded
lengthwise, and lengthwise again,
folding toward the open edge,
so that the union of stars on the blue
field remains outward in full view;
a triangular folding is then begun
at the striped end,
by bringing the corner of the folded edge
to the open edge;
the outer point, turned inward along the open edge,
forms the next triangular fold:
the folding continued so, until the end is reached,
the final corner tucked between
the folds of the blue union,
the form of the folded flag is found to resemble that
of a 3-cornered pouch, or thick cocked hat.

Take this flag, John Glenn, instead of a friend;
instead of a brother, Edward Kennedy, take this flag;
instead of a father, Joe Kennedy, take this flag;
this flag instead of a husband, Ethel Kennedy, take this flag;
this 9-times-folded red-white-striped, star-spotted-blue flag,
tucked and pocketed neatly,
Nation, instead of a leader, take this folded flag.
Robert Kennedy, coffin without coverlet,
beside this hole in the grass,
beside your brother, John Kennedy,
in the grass,
take, instead of a country,
this folded flag;
Robert Kennedy, take this
hole in the grass.

*Arlington Cemetery
June 8, 1968

MAsterMANANiMAl

ANiMAte MANANiMAl MAttress of Nerves
MANipulAtor Motor ANd Motive MAker
MAMMAliAN MAtrix MAt of rivers red
MortAl MANic Morsel Mover shAker

MAteriAl-MAster MAsticAtor oxygeN-eAter
MouNtAiN-MouNter MApper peNetrAtor
iN MoNster MetAl MANtle of the Air
MAssive wAter-surgeoN prestidigitAtor

MAchiNist MAsoN MesoN-Mixer MArble-heAver
coiNer cArver cities-idols-AtoMs-sMAsher
electric lever Metric AlcheMist
MeNtAl AMAzer igNorANt iNcubAtor

cANNibAl AutoMANANiMAl cAllous cAlculAtor
Milky MAgNetic MAN iNNoceNt iNNovAtor
MAlleAble MAMMAl MercuriAl ANd MAteriAl
MAsterANiMAl ANd ANiMA etheriAl

BLEEDING

Stop bleeding   said the knife.
I would if I   could said the cut.
Stop bleeding   you make me messy with this blood.
I'm sorry said   the cut.
Stop or I will   sink in farther said the knife.
Don't said the   cut.
The knife did   not say it couldn't help it but it sank in farther.
If only you   didn't bleed said the knife I wouldn't have to do this.
I know said   the cut I bleed too easily I hate that I can't
help it I   wish I were a knife like you and didn't have to bleed.
Meanwhile stop bleeding will you said the knife.
Yes you   are a mess and sinking in farther said the cut I will
have to   stop.
Have you   stopped by now said the knife.
I've almost   stopped I think.
Why must you bleed in the first place said the knife.
For the reason   maybe that you must do what you must do said the cut.
I can't stand   bleeding said the knife and sank in farther.
I hate it too   said the cut I know it isn't you it's me
you're lucky to   be a knife you ought to be glad about that.
Too many cuts   around said the knife they're messy I don't know
how they stand   themselves.
They don't said   the cut.
You're bleeding   again.
No I've stopped   said the cut. See you're coming out now the
blood is drying   it will rub off you'll be shiny again and clean.
If only cuts   wouldn't bleed so much said the knife coming out a little.
But then knives   might become dull said the cut.
Aren't you bleeding   a little said the knife.
I hope not said the   cut.
I feel you are just   a little.
Maybe just a little   but I can stop now.
I feel a little   wetness still said the knife sinking in
a little but then   coming out a little.
Just a little maybe   just enough said the cut.
That's enough now   stop now do you feel better now said the knife.
I feel I have to   bleed to feel I think said the cut.
I don't I don't have   to feel said the knife drying now becoming shiny.

WOMEN

Women   Or they
   should be   should be
      pedestals   little horses
         moving   those wooden
            pedestals   sweet
               moving   oldfashioned
                  to the   painted
                     motions   rocking
                        of men   horses

               the gladdest things in the toyroom

                  The   feelingly
                     pegs   and then
                     of their   unfeelingly
                  ears   To be
               so familiar   joyfully
            and dear   ridden
         to the trusting   rockingly
      fists   ridden until
To be chafed   the restored

egos dismount and the legs stride away

Immobile   willing
   sweetlipped   to be set
      sturdy   into motion
         and smiling   Women
            women   should be
               should always   pedestals
                  be waiting   to men

OVER THE FIELD

They have a certain beauty, those wheeled
       fish when, steel
       fins stiff out
       from their sides
       they grope

over the field, then through cloud, slice
       silver snouts,
       and climb,

trailing glamorous veils like slime.
Their long abdomens cannot curve, but
       arrogantly cut
       blue,
       power enflaming
       their gills.

       They claim
that sea where no fish swam, until they flew
       to minnow it
       with their metal.

Inflexible bellies carry, like roe,
       Jonahs sitting row
       on row.
       I sit by the fin
       in

one of those whale-big fish, while
several silver minnows, lined up, wheel
       the runway
       way
       below.

ELECTRONIC SOUND

A pebble swells to a boulder at low speed.
                    At 7½ ips a hiss is a hurricane.
                         The basin drain
is Charybdis sucking
                         a clipper down, the ship
                              a paperclip
whirling. Or gargle, brush your teeth, HEAR
                    a winded horse's esophagus lurch
                    on playback at 15/16. Perch
a quarter on edge on a plate, spin:
                    a locomotive's wheel is wrenched loose,
               wobbles down the line to slam the caboose,
keeps on snicking over the ties
                    till it teeters on the embankment,
                         bowls down a cement
ramp, meanders onto the turnpike
                              and into a junkhole
               of scrapped cars. Ceasing to roll,
it shimmies, falters . . .
                         sudden inertia causes
                              pause.
Then a round of echoes
                    descending, a minor yammer
as when a triangle's nicked by the slimmest hammer.

THE JAMES BOND MOVIE

The popcorn is greasy, and I forgot to bring a Kleenex.
A pill that's a bomb inside the stomach of a man inside

The Embassy blows up. Eructations of flame, luxurious
cauliflowers giganticize into motion. The entire 29-ft.

screen is orange, is crackling flesh and brick bursting,
blackening, smithereened. I unwrap a Dentyne and, while

jouncing my teeth in rubber tongue-smarting clove, try
with the 2-inch-wide paper to blot butter off my fingers.

A bubble-bath, room-sized, in which 14 girls, delectable
and sexless, twist-topped Creamy Freezes (their blond,

red, brown, pinkish, lavendar or silver wiglets all
screwed that high, and varnished), scrub-tickle a lone

male, whose chest has just the right amount and distribu-
tion of curly hair. He's nervously pretending to defend

his modesty. His crotch, below the waterline, is also
below the frame—but unsubmerged all 28 slick foamy boobs.

Their makeup fails to let the girls look naked. Caterpil-
lar lashes, black and thick, lush lips glossed pink like

the gum I pop and chew, contact lenses on the eyes that are
mostly blue, they're nose-perfect replicas of each other.

I've got most of the grease off and onto this little square
of paper. I'm folding it now, making creases with my nails.

WEDNESDAY AT THE WALDORF

Two white whales have been installed at
the Waldorf. They are tumbling slowly
above the tables, butting the chandeliers,
submerging, and taking soft bites
out of the red-vested waiters in the
Peacock Room. They are poking *fleur-de-lys*
tails into the long pockets on the
waiters' thighs. They are stealing
breakfast strawberries from two eccentric
guests—one, skunk-cabbage green with
dark peepers—the other, wild rose and
milkweed, barelegged, in Lafayette loafers.
When the two guests enter the elevator,
the whales ascend, bouncing, through all
the ceilings, to the sixth floor. They
get between the sheets. There they turn
candy-pink, with sky-colored eyes, and
silver bubbles start to rise from velvet
navels on the tops of their heads.
Later, a pale blue VW, running on poetry,
weaves down Park Avenue, past yellow
sprouts of forsythia, which, due to dog-do
and dew, are doing nicely. The two
white whales have the blue car in tow
on a swaying chain of bubbles. They are
rising toward the heliport on the Pan Am
roof. There they go, dirigible and slow,
hide-swiping each other, lily tails flipping,
their square velvet snouts stitched with
snug smiles. It is April. "There's
a kind of hush all over the world."

IN THE YARD

Dogwood's snow.
Its ground's air.
Redheaded's riddling
the phone pole.
Fat-tailed she-dog
grinning's thrasher-
red. Oriole there
by the feeder's cheddar
under black bold head.
Neighbor doing yard-
work's getting red.
Lifts tiles to
a barrow. L.I.R.R.'s
four cars rollskate by
white potato blooms
farside the field.
That square's our
bedroom window.
You're not there.
You're away, looking
for nails, or such,
to put up a mirror,
frame the Adam and

Eve, bright hair
held back by the
robin's-egg-blue
band. Or you're at
the body shop about
the broken bumper.
Cabbage butterfly's
found honey, he
thinks, on ring glints
on my hand. I wait
for the ringneck,
who trumpets twice,
parades his mate.
She's gray. Comes
the Blue Bug crunching
driveway. You're back,
barefoot, brought
some fruit. Split me
an apple. We'll
get red, white
halves each, our
juice on the
Indian spread.

CATBIRD IN REDBUD

Catbird in the redbud this morning.
No cat could
mimic that rackety cadenza he's making.
And it's not red,
the trapeze he's swaying on.
After last night's freeze, redbud's violet-pink,
twinkled on by the sun.
That bird's red, though, under the tail he wags,
up sharply, like a wren.
The uncut lawn hides blue violets
with star-gold eyes on the longest stems I've ever seen.
Going to empty the garbage, I simply have to pick some,
reaching to the root of green,
getting my fist dewy,
happening to tear up a dandelion, too.
Lilac, hazy blue-violet, nods buds over the alley fence,
and, like a horse with a yen
for something fresh for breakfast,
I put my nose into a fragrant pompom,
bite off some,
and chew.

FIVE HORSES

Midday, midsummer, the field is watercolor green.
   In the center, slats of an open paddock frame.
   A rusty bathtub for water trough in foreground shade.
   Five horses—two brown, two pinto, one a buckskin—wade

      the wide green. They are made short by the stature
   of the grass—hoofs and half their muzzles unseen.
   They keep the composition balanced by their ease
   and placement. On a rectangle of sun, the two brown
   backs, like polished tables, solid, reddish rove.

      The black-on-whites, turned hinders to the wood,
         necks down, feel a slow breeze drag the scarves
      of their manes aslant. One's whole head is a dark hood
         through which the ears, unpainted, point. The other's a mare
         with astonishing blue eyes, and all blond, except for a pale

   tan patch over stifle and loin. The buckskin, youngest,
   crops in shade alone, tail thrown over tawny rump
   in a constant feathery rotor against flies.
   They move and munch so gradually, the scene
   seems not to change: clean colors outlined on mat-green,

         under a horizontal wash of steady blue
            that ink-sharp darker swallows, distant, dip into.
         That pasture was the end of one of our walks.
            We brought carrots that we broke and passed
            on the flats of our hands, to the lips of Buck and Blue,

      to Spook, Brown I and Brown II, who nipped and jostled
         each other over the gate to get them.
      They'd wait while we stroked their forelocks and smooth jaws.
      I could look into the square pupils of the palfrey, Blue,
   her underlip and nostrils, like a rabbit's, pink.

         Pied spots, as on a cheetah, showed faint under the hair
         of Buck, your horse: you liked him best.
            Close up, we rubbed the ragged streaks and stars on their
            foreheads and chests, slapped their muscular necks,
               while they nudged us, snuffling our pockets for more.

      Now we've gone past summer and the green field, but I could draw
         their profiles, so distinguished the five faces stay in view,
      leaning over the gate boards toward our coming,
   waiting for carrots, staring, yearning in a row.

BLUE

Blue, but you are Rose, too,
and buttermilk, but with blood
dots showing through.
A little salty your white
nape boy-wide. Glinting hairs
shoot back of your ears' Rose
that tongue likes to feel
the maze of, slip into the funnel,
tell a thunder-whisper to.
When I kiss, your eyes' straight
lashes down crisp go like doll's
blond straws. Glazed iris Roses,
your lids unclose to Blue-ringed
targets, their dark sheen-spokes
almost green. I sink in Blue-
black Rose-heart holes until you
blink. Pink lips, the serrate
folds taste smooth, and Rosehip-
round, the center bud I suck.
I milknip your two Blue-skeined
blown Rose beauties, too, to sniff
their berries' blood, up stiff
pink tips. You're white in
patches, only mostly Rose,
buckskin and salty, speckled
like a sky. I love your spots,
your white neck, Rose, your hair's
wild straw splash, silk spools
for your ears. But where white
spouts out, spills on your brow
to clear eyepools, wheel shafts
of light, Rose, you are Blue.

YEAR OF THE DOUBLE SPRING

Passing a lank boy, bangs to the eyebrows,
licking a Snow Flake cone, and cones on the tulip tree
   up stiff, honeysuckle tubelets weighting a vine,
and passing *Irene Gay—Realtor, The Black Whale, Rexall,*
   and others—(Irene, don't sue me, it's just your sign
I need in the scene)—
   remembering lilac a month back, a different faded shade,
buying a paper with the tide table instead of the twister
   forecast on page three,
then walking home from the village, beneath the viaduct,
   I find Midwest echoes answering echoes
that another, yet the same train, wakes here out East.
   I'm thinking of how I leaned on you, you leaning
in the stone underpass striped with shadows of tracks
   and ties, and I said, "Give me a kiss, A.D.,
even if you are tranquilized," and I'm thinking
   of the Day of the Kingfisher, the Indigo Day of the Bunting,
of the Catfish Night I locked the keys in the car
   and you tried to jimmy in, but couldn't, with a clothes hanger.
The night of the juke at Al's—*When Something's Wrong*
   With My Baby—you pretended to flake out on the bench,
and I poured icy Scotch into the thimble of your belly,
   lifting the T-shirt. Another night you threw up
in a Negro's shoe. It's Accabonac now instead of
   Tippecanoe. I'm remembering how we used to drive
to *The Custard* "to check out the teenage boxes."
   I liked the ones around the Hondas, who
from a surly distance, from under the hair in their eyes,
   cruised the girls in flowered shorts.
One day back there, licking cones, we looked in
   on a lioness lying with her turd behind the gritty window
of a little zoo. I liked it there. I'd like it
   anywhere with you.
Here there are gorgeous pheasants, no hogs, blond horses,
   and Alec Guiness seen at *The Maidstone* Memorial Eve—
and also better dumps. You scavenged my plywood desk top,
   a narrow paint-flecked old door, and the broad white
wicker I'm sitting in now.

While you're at the dump hunting for more—
maybe a double spring good as that single you climbed to
    last night (and last year)—I sit in front of a house,
remembering a house back there, thinking of a house—
    where? when?—by spring next year?
I notice the immature oak leaves, vivid as redbud almost,
    and shaped like the spoor of the weasel we saw
once by the Wabash.
    Instead of "to the *Readmore*" riffling *Playboy,* I found
you yesterday in that Newtown Lane newspaper store
    I don't yet know the name of. Stay with me, A.D.,
don't blow. Scout out that bed. Go find tennis
    instead of squash mates, surfboarders, volleyball
boys to play with. I know you will, before long—
    maybe among the lifeguards—big, cool-coned,
straight-hipped, stander-on-one-finger, strong.

CAMOUFLEUR

Walked in the swamp   His cheek vermilion
            A dazzling prince
    Neck-band white   Cape he trailed
            Metallic mottled
Over rain-rotted leaves   Wet mud reflected
            Waded olive water
    His opulent gear   Pillars of the reeds
            Parted the strawgold
        Brilliance   Made him disappear

Unconscious
came a beauty to my
wrist
and stopped my pencil,
merged its shadow profile with
my hand's ghost
on the page:
Red Spotted Purple or else Mourning
Cloak,
paired thin-as-paper wings, near black,
were edged on the seam side poppy orange,
as were its spots.

UNCONSCIOUS

CAME A BEAUTY

I sat arrested, for its soot-haired
body's worm
shone in the sun.
It bent its tongue long as
a leg
black on my skin
and clung without my
feeling,
while its tomb-stained
duplicate parts of
a window opened.
And then I
moved.

THE BLUE BOTTLE

"Go
to the other
shore
and return,"
I wrote
in a note
to the bottle,
and put it in it.
It kept it
dry.
I could see
through
the blue
bottle blue
notepaper
with blue ink
words.
The cork was tight.
It might
make it.
Blue wavelets let
it go,
began to
take it.
Oh,
it hobbled
beyond the jetty
rocks barnacled
and snailed.
It bobbled,
snagged
on a crag,
wagged
with its butt

end butted,
but sailed
so far that
its glass
had to pass
for glitter,
among glitters,
on the flat
glass
of the bay
and my
eye-
glass.
Baited
with
words
and weighted,
I thought,
"It will get away.
Get away
with it!" I
thought,
watching
the laps,
the lapse,
listening
to the lisp,
the lips
of the bay-
mouth
making shore,
making sure
every rock got
rounded

a little more
today,
every pebble
pounded,
brought
to ground
and rounded,
to be gritted
to a grain
someday,
some sum-day
to be mounded
into rock again.
Some fishermen
were fishing
with little
fishes hooked
to hook
bigger fish.
And some they caught
and cooked.
And some they
put on bigger
hooks to get
bigger fishes yet.
And all day
the bay
smacked
its lips, big
and little,
rocking big and
little ships,
that smacked
and rocked like

oyster crackers
in a dish.
The tide
was either going
out or it
was coming in.
Not for an in-
stant could it stop,
since its pulse
compels
it, and since
the syndrome swells.
Since syn-rhythm
rules all motion,
and motion makes
erosion,
all that's munched
apart and
swallowed
shifts, collects, is
heaped and hollowed,
heaped and
hollowed, heaped
and hollowed.
All
the little
waves I
followed
out to where my
bottle wallowed.
I was sure, sure, sure,
I was shore,
shore it would endure,
endure,
would obey, obey
internal pulsion,
pulsion

of the bay,
would turn, turn,
return, return
with the turn-
turn-turn-
ing glassy floor
that bore
it, for
it wore
internal or-
der at its core.
Constantly
my eye
did pass
over blue,
looking
with blue,
for bluer
blue
on the bottle-
blue bay-glass.
When tide re-
turned,
when shore re-
stored,
my bottle's envelope
of glass
would
be re-
versed,
even though
its core
burst.
First
erosion,
then corrosion,
then assemblage.

It would be
nursed
again to
vessel-shape,
transparent float,
hard, hollow
bladder,
transferred
transplant,
holder of my note.
In what
language, then,
the words,
the words within
its throat?
What answer?
What other-colored
ink?
My blue
eye,
thinking,
thinking, blinked.
My
eye, my
I
lost link
with the blue
chink,
with crinkled
wavelets-lets-lets
let it, rising,
racing, wrinkling,
falling,
be swallowed
in that inkling,
let it
sink.

HOW EVERYTHING HAPPENS (Based on a Study of the Wave)

                                              happen.
                                          to
                                        up
                                  stacking
                                is
                            something
When nothing is happening

When it happens
                something
                        pulls
                            back
                                not
                                    to
                                      happen.

When   has happened.
      pulling back   stacking up
                    happens

              has happened   stacks up.
When it   something   nothing
                        pulls back while

Then nothing is happening.

                                      happens.
                                  and
                            forward
                        pushes
                      up
                  stacks
            something
Then

119

ZERO
IN THE COVE

The waves have frozen
in their tracks and turned
to snow, and into ice

the snow has turned, become
the shore. Where in soft
summer sand burned by

water flat, paralytic
breakers stand hurled
into a ridge of ice. Ice
fattens about the poles
that told the tide.
Their two shadows point

out stiff behind them on a dead
floor, thickened and too rough
for light to glass,

as if the moon were drained
of power, and water
were unknown. The cove

is locked, a still
chest. Depth itself has
died with its
reflection
lost.

from Half Sun Half Sleep

COLORS WITHOUT OBJECTS

Colors without objects—colors alone—
wriggle in the tray of my eye,
incubated under the great flat lamp of the sun:
bodiless blue, little razor-streak,
yellow melting like a firework petal,
double purple yo-yo in a broth of murky gold.
Sharp green squints I have never seen
minnow-dive the instant they're alive.
Bulb-reds with flickering cilia
dilate, but then implode to disks of impish
scotomata, that flee into the void.
Weird orange slats of hot thought
about to make a basket find no material here.
They slim to a snow of needles, are erased.
Now a mottling takes place. All colors fix
chromosomic links that dexterously mix,
flip, exchange their aerial ladders.
Such stunts of speed and metamorphosis
breed impermanent, objectless acts—
a thick, a brilliant bacteria—
but most do not survive. I wait for a few
iridium specks of idea to thrive
in the culture of my eye.

THE BLINDMAN

The blindman placed
a tulip on his tongue for purple's taste.
Cheek to grass, his green

was rough excitement's sheen
of little whips.
In water to his lips

he named the sea blue and white,
the basin of his tears and fallen beads of sight.
He said: This scarf is red;

I feel the vectors to its thread
that dance down from the sun. I know
the seven fragrances of the rainbow.

I have caressed
the orange hair of flames. Pressed
to my ear,

a pomegranate lets me hear
crimson's flute.
Trumpets tell me yellow. Only ebony is mute.

THE KITE

Triangular face, or mask,
dangling a spinal cord,

or like the diagram of a spirochete,
the tail wiggling.

Desperate paper pollywog, aloft,
pushing upstream,

alive because wind pours over, under
it, like water.

The sky with invisible wind,
the frame of Being around a face,

behind the unprobed surface
the mirror's space.

"Perhaps all things are inanimate
and it is the void that lives,"

I think, until I remember
that a string,

not seen in the white air,
is tied to a finger below.

The paper face is fixed
in a magnetic flow

on which it depends,
by which it is repelled.

The tug of the void,
the will of the world

together declare
placement for the shivering mask.

THE TALL FIGURES OF GIACOMETTI

We move by means of our mud bumps.
We bubble as do the dead but more slowly.

The products of excruciating purges
we are squeezed out thin hard and dry.

If we exude a stench it is petrified sainthood.
Our feet are large crude fused together

solid like anvils. Ugly as truth is ugly
we are meant to stand upright a long time

and shudder without motion
under the scintillating pins of light

that dart between our bodies
of pimpled mud and your eyes.

ALL THAT TIME

I saw two trees embracing.
One leaned on the other
as if to throw her down.
But she was the upright one.
Since their twin youth, maybe she
had been pulling him toward her
all that time,

and finally almost uprooted him.
He was the thin, dry, insecure one,
the most wind-warped, you could see.
And where their tops tangled
it looked like he was crying
on her shoulder.
On the other hand, maybe he

had been trying to weaken her,
break her, or at least
make her bend
over backwards for him
just a little bit.
And all that time
she was standing up to him

the best she could.
She was the most stubborn,
the straightest one, that's a fact.
But he had been willing
to change himself—
even if it was for the worse—
all that time.

At the top they looked like one
tree, where they were embracing.
It was plain they'd be
always together.
Too late now to part.
When the wind blew, you could hear
them rubbing on each other.

A CITY GARDEN IN APRIL

The Magnolia
In the shade
each tight cone

untwists to a goblet.
Under light

the rim widens,
splits like silk.
Seven spatulate

white flakes
float open, purple
dregs at the nape.

The Old Ailanthus
Impossible to count
your fingers,

and all of them crooked.
How many tips

intending further tender
tips, in rigid grapple-

clusters weave with the
wind, with the shift

of the puffy rain cloud?
With the first big

honey-heat of the sun
you'll unloose

your secret explosion.
Then impossible to count

all the lubricious torches
in your labyrinth of arms.

Daffodils
Yellow telephones
in a row in the garden
are ringing,
shrill with light.

Old-fashioned spring
brings earliest models out
each April the same,
naïve and classical.

Look into the yolk-
colored mouthpieces
alert with echoes.
Say hello to time.

The Little Fountain

The sun's force
and the fountain's

cool hypnosis—
opposed purities

begin their marathon.
Colorless and motionful

the bowl feels twirl
a liquid hub,

the soft, incessant wheel
slurs over marble

until the dilation frays,
dribbling crystal strings.

The circle encircled,
the reborn circle

synchronized,
repeats the friction,

plash and whisper,
as of feathers rubbed

together or glossy hair.
Bounced from the sun's

breastplate, fierce colors
of flowers, fat leaves,

flinching birds—
while the gray dial

of water keeps all day
its constancy and flicker.

The Vine

You've put out
new nooses since
yesterday.

With a hook and
a hook and a hook
you took territory

over brick,
seized that side
and knitted

outward to snare
the air with knots
and nipples of leaves.

Your old rope-root,
gray and dried,
made us think you'd

died self-strangled.
One day you inflated
a green parachute,

then breezily invented
a tent, and in five
you've proliferated

a whole plumed pavilion.
Not only alive
but splurging

up and out like a geyser.
Old Faithful,
it's worth a winter

hung up stiff
in sullen petrifaction
for such excess.

DEAR ELIZABETH*

Yes, I'd like a pair of *Bicos de Lacre*—
meaning beaks of "lacquer" or "sealing wax"?
(the words are the same in Portuguese)
". . . about 3 inches long including the tail,
red bills and narrow bright red masks . . ."
You say the male has a sort of "drooping
mandarin-mustache—one black stripe"—

otherwise the sexes are alike. "Tiny but
plump, shading from brown and gray on top
to pale beige, white, and a rose red spot
on the belly"—their feathers, you tell
me, incredibly beautiful "alternating
lights and darks like nearly invisible
wave-marks on a sandflat at low tide,

and with a pattern so fine one must put on
reading glasses to appreciate it properly."
Well, do they sing? If so, I expect their
note is extreme. Not something one hears,
but must watch the cat's ears to detect.
And their nest, that's "smaller than a fist,
with a doorway in the side just wide enough

for each to get into to sleep." They must
be very delicate, not easy to keep. Still,
on the back porch on Perry St., here, I'd
build them a little Brazil. I'd save every
shred and splinter of New York sunshine
and work through the winter to weave them
a bed. A double, exactly their size,

*A reply to Elizabeth Bishop in Brazil.

130

with a roof like the Ark. I'd make sure to
leave an entrance in the side. I'd set it
in among the morning-glories where the
gold-headed flies, small as needles' eyes,
are plentiful. Although "their egg is apt
to be barely as big as a baked bean . . ."
It rarely hatches in captivity, you mean—

but we could hope! In today's letter you
write, "The *Bicos de Lacre* are adorable as
ever—so tiny, neat, and taking baths
constantly in this heat, in about ¼ inch
of water—then returning to their *filthy*
little nest to lay another egg—which
never hatches." But here it might! And it

doesn't matter that "their voice is weak,
they have no song." I can see them as I
write—on their perch on my porch. "From
the front they look like a pair of half-
ripe strawberries"—except for that stripe.
"At night the cage looks empty" just as
you say. I have "a moment's fright"—

then see the straw nest moving softly.
Yes, dear Elizabeth, if you would be so
kind, I'd like a pair of *Bicos de Lacre*—
especially as in your P.S. you confess,
"I already have two unwed female wild
canaries, for which I must find husbands
in order to have a little song around here."

MOTHERHOOD

She sat on a shelf,
her breasts two bellies
on her poked-out belly,
on which the navel looked
like a sucked-in mouth—
her knees bent and apart,
her long left arm raised,
with the large hand knuckled
to a bar in the ceiling—
her right hand clamping
the skinny infant to her chest—
its round, pale, new,
soft muzzle hunting
in the brown hair for a nipple,
its splayed, tiny hand picking
at her naked, dirty ear.
Twisting its little neck,
with tortured, ecstatic eyes
the size of lentils, it looked
into her severe, close-set,
solemn eyes, that beneath bald
eyelids glared—dull lights
in sockets of leather.

She twitched some chin-hairs,
with pain or pleasure,
as the baby-mouth found and
yanked at her nipple;
its pink-nailed, jointless
fingers, wandering her face,
tangled in the tufts
of her cliffy brows.
She brought her big
hand down from the bar—
with pretended exasperation
unfastened the little hand,
and locked it within her palm—
while her right hand,

with snag-nailed forefinger
and short, sharp thumb, raked
the new orange hair
of the infant's skinny flank—
and found a louse,
which she lipped, and
thoughtfully crisped
between broad teeth.
She wrinkled appreciative
nostrils which, without a nose,
stood open—damp holes
above the poke of her mouth.

She licked her lips, flicked
her leather eyelids—
then, suddenly flung
up both arms and grabbed
the bars overhead.
The baby's scrabbly fingers
instantly caught the hair—
as if there were metal rings there—
in her long, stretched armpits.
And, as she stately swung,
and then proudly, more swiftly
slung herself from corner
to corner of her cell—
arms longer than her round
body, short knees bent—
her little wild-haired,
poke-mouthed infant hung,
like some sort of trophy,
or decoration, or shaggy medal—
shaped like herself—but new,
clean, soft and shining
on her chest.

FOUR-WORD LINES

Your eyes are just
like bees, and I
feel like a flower.
Their brown power makes
a breeze go over
my skin. When your
lashes ride down and
rise like brown bees'
legs, your pronged gaze
makes my eyes gauze.
I wish we were
in some shade and
no swarm of other
eyes to know that
I'm a flower breathing
bare, laid open to
your bees' warm stare.
I'd let you wade
in me and seize
with your eager brown
bees' power a sweet
glistening at my core.

SWIMMERS

Tossed
by the muscular sea,
we are lost,
and glad to be lost
in troughs of rough

love. A bath in
laughter, our dive
into foam,
our upslide and float
on the surf of desire.

But sucked to the root
of the water-mountain—
immense—
about to tip upon us
the terror of total

delight—
we are towed,
helpless in its
swell, by hooks
of our hair;

then dangled, let go,
made to race—
as the wrestling chest
of the sea, itself
tangled, tumbles

in its own embrace.
Our limbs like eels
are water-boned,
our faces lost
to difference and

contour, as the lapping
crests.
They cease
their charge,
and rock us

in repeating hammocks
of the releasing
tide—
until supine we glide,
on cool green

smiles
of an exhaling
gladiator,
to the shore
of sleep.

NAKED IN BORNEO
(From a painting by Tobias)

They wear air
or water like a skin,
their skin the smoothest suit.
Are tight and loose
as the leopard, or sudden
and still as the moccasin.
Their blouse is black

shadows of fronds
on a copper vest of sun.
Glossy rapids are
their teeth and eyes
beneath straight harsh blonds
of rained-on grain that thatch
their round head-huts.

Long thongs their bodies, bows
or canoes. Both tense and lax
their bodies, spears
they tool, caress, hoard, decorate
with cuts. Their fears
are their weapons. Coiled or
straight they run up trees

and on jungle thorns; their feet
are their shoes, fierce hair
their hats that hold off sun's hate.
They glide, muscles of water
through water, dark oil-beads
pave their lashing
torsos. Are bare in air,

are wind-combed, armpit and groin;
are taut arrows turned sinuous reeds
for dancing on drumskin ground.
Rasped by the sun's tongue, then moon-licked
all their slick
moist feathered shafts
in the hammocks of tangled thighs

the silks of night plash among.
Their joys, their toys are their children
who like kittens ride
their mother's neck, or wrestle
with the twins of her breasts
where she squats by the meal pot.
At hunter's naked side

little hunter stalks fix-eyed,
miniature poison-dart
lifted, learning the game:
young pointer in the bush,
fish-diver in the river,
grave apprentice in the art
of magic pain

when the blood pines
to be let a little,
to sharpen the friction of Alive,
in the feckless skin
leave some slits and signs
that old spirit leaked out,
new spirit sneaked in.

THE PREGNANT DREAM

I had a dream in which I had a
dream,
and in my dream I told you,
"Listen, I will tell you my
dream." And I began to tell you. And
you told me, "I haven't time to listen while you tell your
dream."

Then in my dream I
dreamed I began to
forget my
dream.
And I forgot my
dream.
And I began to tell you, "Listen, I have
forgot my
dream."
And now I tell you: "Listen while I tell you my
dream, a
dream
in which I dreamed I
forgot my
dream,"
and I begin to tell you: "In my dream you told me, 'I haven't time to
listen.'"

And you tell me: "You dreamed I wouldn't
listen to a
dream that you
forgot?
I haven't time to listen to
forgotten
dreams."

"But I haven't   forgot I
                 dreamed," I tell you,
            "a   dream in which I told you,
                 'Listen, I have
                 forgot,' and you told me, 'I haven't time.'"
"I haven't time," you tell me.

And now I begin to   forget that I
                      forgot what I began to tell you in my
                      dream.
And I tell you,   "Listen,
                      listen, I begin to
                      forget."

UNTITLED

I   will   be   earth   you   be   the   flower
You   have   found   my   root   you   are   the   rain
I   will   be   boat   and   you   the   rower
You   rock   you   toss   me   you   are   the   sea
How   be   steady   earth   that's   now   a   flood
The   root's   the   oar's   afloat   where's   blown   our   bud
We   will   be   desert   pure   salt   the   seed
Burn   radiant   sex   born   scorpion   need

CAUSE & EFFECT

Am I the bullet
or the target,
or the hand
that holds the gun?
Or the whisper
in the brain saying *Aim, Fire?*
Is the bullet innocent though it kill?
Must the target stand unblinking and still?
Can one escape, the other stop, if it will?
Will the trigger-finger obey through force?
If the hand reverse command,
will the pregnant gun abort its curse?
The brain,
the brain, surely it can refrain,
unclench the gun, break open
the pod of murder,
let the target rise and run.
But first, the whisper must be caught,
before the shot,
the single wasp be burnt out,
before the nest, infested, swarms with
the multiple thought,
each sting the trigger pressed.

FABLE FOR WHEN THERE'S NO WAY OUT

Grown too big for his skin,
and it grown hard,

without a sea and atmosphere—
he's drunk it all up—

his strength's inside him now,
but there's no room to stretch.

He pecks at the top
but his beak's too soft;

though instinct or ambition shoves,
he can't get through.

Barely old enough to bleed
and already bruised!

In a case this tough
what's the use

if you break your head
instead of the lid?

Despair tempts him
to just go limp:

Maybe the cell's
already a tomb,

and beginning end
in this round room.

Still, stupidly he pecks
and pecks, as if from under

his own skull—
yet makes no crack . . .

No crack until
he finally cracks,

and kicks and stomps.
What a thrill

and shock to feel
his little gaff poke

through the floor!
A way he hadn't known or meant.

Rage works if reason won't.
When locked up, bear down.

WHILE SEATED IN A PLANE

On a kicked-up floor of cloud
a couch of cloud, deformed and fluffy;
far out, more celestial furniture—fat chairs

slowly puffing forth their airy stuffing.
On dream-feet I walked into that large
parlor on cool pearl—but found it far

between the restless resting places.
Pinnacles, detaching, floating from their bases,
swelled to turbulent beds and tables,

ebbed to ebullient chairs,
then footstools that, degraded,
flowed with the floor before I could get there.

One must be a cloud to occupy a house of cloud.
I twirled in my dream, and was deformed
and reformed, making many faces,

refusing the fixture of a solid soul.
So came to a couch I could believe,
although it altered

its facile carvings, at each heave
became another throne.
Neither dissolved nor solid, I was settled

and unsettled in my placeless chair.
A voluntary mobile, manybodied, I traded
shape for the versatility of air.

FLYING HOME FROM UTAH

Forests are branches of a tree lying down,
its blurred trunk in the north.
Farms are fitted pieces of a floor,

tan and green tiles that get smoother,
smaller, the higher we fly.
Heel-shaped dents of water I know are deep

from here appear opaque, of bluish glass.
Curl after curl, rivers are coarse locks
unraveling southward over the land;

hills, rubbed felt, crumpled bumps
of antlers pricking from young bucks' heads.
Now towns are scratches here and there

on a wide, brown-bristled hide.
Long roads rayed out from the sores of cities
begin to fester and crawl with light—

above them the plane is a passing insect
that eyes down there remark, forget
in the moment it specks the overcast.

It climbs higher. Clouds become ground.
Pillows of snow meet, weld into ice.
Alone on a moonlit stainless rink

glides the ghost of a larva, the shadow
of our plane. Lights go on
in the worm-belly where we sit;

it becomes the world, and seems to cease
to travel—only vibrates, stretched out tense
in the tank of night.

The room of my mind replaces the long, lit room.
I dream I point my eye over a leaf
and fascinate my gaze upon its veins:

A sprawled leaf, many-fingered, its radial
ridges limber, green—but curled,
tattered, pocked, the brown palm

nibbled by insects, nestled in by worms:
One leaf of a tree that's one tree of a forest,
that's the branch of the vein of a leaf

of a tree. Perpetual worlds
within, upon, above the world, the world
a leaf within a wilderness of worlds.

GODS | CHILDREN

They are born naked,
and without tails.
They cannot fly.
Their blood is red.
They are children until they die,
and then "are God's children."
Are gods . . . children . . .
Are *gods children?*

Worlds are their heads,
oceans infants' serene eyes.
Blue and green they invented.
Leaves did not grow
or the wind blow
until their spine
lifted like a tendril.
Their tongue curled.
Their hand made a sign.

They are not like fruit
though their skin is sweet.
Though they rot they have wrought
the numbers one to ten.
They founded the sun.
When the sun found them
it undertook its path and aim.
The moon, also,
when it received its name.
The air first heard itself called glory
in their lungs.

Beasts they placed in the sky
and in their caves
and on their platforms,
for they remembered their cradles,
their blood in flow
told them their beginnings.
The beloved hoofs,
massy necks,

rich nostrils,
sex, a red coal in the groin,
they worshipped.
Also their helical rod
called evil and sapience.

They ensorcelled angels,
dreamed queerer forms,
on the brain's map fixed a junction, "Infinity,"
in the entrail's maze, "Prophecy,"
and made "Measure"
and the dance of "The Particles,"
with a switch the system, "Time," turned on,
a braided chain,
torque for the whole of space
their game.

They play,
are flexible jugglers and jongleurs,
fashioners of masks;
are mirror-makers
and so dupe themselves,
dress themselves,
are terrified at flesh,
think each other phantoms,
idols, demons, toys;
make of each other handles, ladders, quicksands;
are to each other houses of safety,
hammocks of delight.

They cannot fly,
but nest themselves in bullets
and, dressed as embryos,
shoot out to a circle beyond their ball.
And can breathe with such a placenta,
their foot floating
far separate from its ground.

Before, in iron capsules
lived under the sea,
in baskets inflated rode the air.
Many other marvels built besides.
Are mysterious charts

beneath their skulls' membranes.
And have invented madness.

Under their bodies' casings
in intricate factories
work their strong, soft engines.
Their blood is red.
Color and name they invented,
and so created it.
And have named themselves.

And it is even so
that they operate upon one another,
and increase,
and make replicas,
and replace one another,
new for old,
and tick to death
like moments.

When they are dead,
they are made naked,
are washed and dressed.
They do this for each other
like children.
And are fixed into fine boxes
like children fix their dolls.

And then?
"Are God's children."
Are gods . . . children . . .
Then are gods children?

AT TRURO

The sea is unfolding scrolls
and rolling them up again.
It is an ancient diary

the waves are murmuring.
The words are white curls,
great capitals are seen

on the wrinkled swells.
Repeated rhythmically
it seems to me I read

my own biography.
Once I was a sea bird.
With beak a sharp pen,

I drew my signature on air.
There is a chapter when,
a crab, I slowly scratched

my name on a sandy page,
and once, a coral, wrote
a record of my age

on the wall of a water-grotto.
When I was a sea worm
I never saw the sun,

but flowed, a salty germ,
in the bloodstream of the sea.
There I left an alphabet

but it grew dim to me.
Something caught me in its net,
took me from the deep

book of the ocean, weaned me,
put fin and wing to sleep,
made me stand and made me

face the sun's dry eye.
On the shore of intellect
I forgot how to fly

above the wave, below it.
When I touched my foot
to land's thick back,

it stuck like stem or root.
In brightness I lost track
of my underworld

of ultraviolet wisdom.
My fiery head furled
up its cool kingdom

and put night away.
The sea is unfolding scrolls,
and rolling them up.

As if the sun were blind
again I feel the suck
of the sea's dark mind.

THE LIGHTNING

The lightning waked me. It slid unde r
my eyelid. A black book flipped ope n
to an illuminated page. Then insta ntly
shut. Words of destiny were being ut-
tered in the distance. If only I could
make them out! . . . Next day, as I lay
in the sun, a symbol for concei ving the
universe was scratched on my e yeball.
But quickly its point eclipse d, and
softened, in the scabbard of my brain.

My cat speaks one word: Fo ur vowels
and a consonant. He rece ives with the
hairs of his body the wh ispers of the
stars. The kinglet spe aks by flashing
into view a ruby feath er on his head.
He is held by a threa d to the eye of
the sun and cannot fall into error.
Any flower is a per fect ear, or else it
is a thousand lips . . . When will I grope
clear of the entr ails of intellect?

OUT OF THE SEA, EARLY

A bloody
egg yolk. A burnt hole
spreading in a sheet. An en-
raged rose threatening to bloom.
A furnace hatchway opening, roaring.
A globular bladder filling with immense
juice. I start to scream. A red hydrocepha-
lic head is born, teetering on the stump of
its neck. When it separates, it leaks rasp-
berry from the horizon down the wide esca-
lator. The cold blue boiling waves cannot
scour out that band, that broadens, slid-
ing toward me up the wet sand slope. The
fox-hair grows, grows thicker on the
upfloating head. By six o'clock,
diffused to ordinary gold,
it exposes each silk thread and rumple in the carpet.

THE WAVE AND THE DUNE

The wave-shaped dune is still.
Its curve does not break,
though it looks as if it will,

like the head of the dune-
shaped wave advancing,
its ridge strewn

with white shards flaking.
A sand-faced image of the wave
is always in the making.

Opposite the sea's rough glass
cove, the sand's smooth-whittled cave,
under the brow of grass,

is sunny and still. Rushing
to place its replica
on the shore, the sea is pushing

sketches of itself
incessantly into the foreground.
All the models smash upon the shelf,

but grain by grain the creeping sand
reërects their profiles
and makes them stand.

SLEEPING OVERNIGHT ON THE SHORE

Earth turns
        one cheek to the sun
while the other tips
        its crags and dimples into shadow.
We say sun comes up,
        goes down,
but it is our planet's incline
        on its shy invisible neck.
The smooth skin of the sea,
        the bearded buttes of the land
blush orange,
        we say it is day.
Then earth in its turning
        slips half of itself away
from the ever burning.
        Night's frown
smirches earth's face,
        by those hours marked older.
It is dark, we say.
        But night is a fiction
hollowed at the back of our ball,
        when from its obverse side
a cone of self-thrown shade
        evades the shining,
and black and gray
        the cinema of dreams streams through
our sandgrain skulls
        lit by our moon's outlining.

Intermittent moon
        that we say climbs
or sets, circles only.
        Earth flicks it past its shoulder.
It tugs at the teats of the sea.
        And sky
is neither high
        nor is earth low.

There is no dark
            but distance
between stars.
            No dawn,
for it is always day
            on Gas Mountain, on the sun—
and horizon's edge
            the frame of our eye.

Cool sand on which we lie
            and watch the gray waves
clasp, unclasp
            a restless froth of light,
silver saliva of the sucking moon—
            whose sun is earth
who's moon to the sun—
            To think this shore,
each lit grain plain
            in the foot-shaped concaves
heeled with shadow,
            is pock or pocket
on an aging pin
            that juggler sun once threw,
made twirl among
            those other blazing objects out
around its crown.
            And from that single toss
the Nine still tumble—
            swung in a carousel of staring light,
where each rides ringleted
            by its pebble-moons—
white lumps of light
            that are never to alight,
for there is no down.

MODELS OF THE UNIVERSE

1

At moment X
the universe began.
It began at point X.
Since then,
through the Hole in a Nozzle,
stars have spewed. An
inexhaustible gush
populates the void forever.

2

The universe was there
before time ran.
A grain
slipped in the glass:
the past began.
The Container
of the Stars expands;
the sand
of matter multiplies forever.

3

From zero radius
to a certain span,
the universe, a Large Lung
specked with stars,
inhales time
until, turgid, it can
hold no more,
and collapses. Then
space breathes, and inhales again,
and breathes again: Forever.

OF ROUNDS

MOON
　　　round
　　　　　goes around while going around a
　　　　　　　　　　　　　　　round
　　　　　　　　　　　　　　　EARTH
EARTH
　　　round
　　　　　with MOON
　　　　　　　　round
　　　　　　　　　going around while going around
goes around while going around a
　　　　　　　　round
　　　　　　　　SUN
SUN
　　　round
　　　　　with EARTH
　　　　　　　　round
　　　　　　　　　with MOON
　　　　　　　　　　　round
　　　　　　　　　　　going around while going
around, and MERCURY
　　　　　　　　round
　　　　　　　　　and VENUS
　　　　　　　　　　round
　　　　　　　　　　going around while
going around, and MARS
　　　　　　　　round
　　　　　　　　with two MOONS
　　　　　　　　　　　round
　　　　　　　　　　　round
　　　　　　　　　　　　going around
while going around, and JUPITER
　　　　　　　　round
　　　　　　　　with fourteen MOONS
　　　　　　　　　　　　round
　　　　　　　　　　　　round
　　　　　　　　　　　　round
　　　　　　　　　　　　round
　　　　　　　　　　　　round
　　　　　　　　　　　　round
　　　　　　　　　　　　round
　　　　　　　　　　　　round
　　　　　　　　　　　　round
　　　　　　　　　　　　round
　　　　　　　　　　　　round
　　　　　　　　　　　　round
　　　　　　　　　　　　round
　　　　　　　　　　　　round

going around while going around, and SATURN

           round

            with ten

MOONS

   round

   round

   round

   round

   round

   round

   round

   round

   round

   round

     going around while going around, and URANUS

              round

with five MOONS

    round

    round

    round

    round

    round

    going around while going around, and NEPTUNE

round

  with two MOONS

     round

     round

     going around while going around, and

PLUTO

  round

   going around while going around, goes around while

going around

   A   OF ROUNDS

        Round

AFTER THE FLIGHT OF RANGER 7

Moon, old fossil,
to be scrubbed
and studied like
a turtle's stomach,
prodded over
on your back,

invulnerable hump
that stumped us,
pincers prepare to
pick your secrets,
bludgeons of light
to force your seams.

Old fossil, glistening
in the continuous rain
of meteorites
blown to you from
between the stars,
stilt feet mobilize

to alight upon you,
ticking feelers
determine your fissures,
to impact a pest
of electric eggs
in the cracks

of your cold
volcanoes. Tycho,
Copernicus, Kepler,
look for geysers,
strange abrasions,
zodiacal wounds.

AUGUST 19, PAD 19

. . . . 8 days without weighing anything.
Not knowing up from down.
Positioned for either breech birth
or urn burial. My mission the practice
of catching up by slowing down,
I am the culmination of a 10-storey bottle,
in 3 disconnectable parts,
being fueled with seething vapor
becoming water becoming fire.
I am the throbbing cork about to pop.

. . . . About to be dragged backward
through 121 sunsets,
not to bathe or drink bare light raw air.
My $75 pencil in my grotesque hand
prepares to float above the clipboard
strapped to my right knee.

. . . . T minus 10 and counting.
Over my obsolete epiderm redundant with
hairs and pits of moisture
I wear my new, rich, inflatable skin,
the bicep patch a proud tattoo,
a galaxy of 50 States,
my telemetric skull, a glossy cupola
resembling the glans of an Aztec god.
My sliding jaw, my safe transparent face
closes. Lungs, you will learn
to breathe hydrogen.

. . . . T minus 10 and counting.
Belted and bolted in, the capsule plugged,
when my 2 umbilical hoses tear free,
I shall increase to the bulk of 7 men,
be halfway to Africa in 12 minutes,
40 seconds. A bead beyond the bulge of earth,
extruded, banished. Till hooked to

the swivel of my ellipse,
I'm played through day and night and east
and west, reeled between apogee and perigee.

. . . . The erector stiffly swoons to its
concrete grave.

. . . . T minus 10 and holding.
Below in the blockhouse, pressed to the
neck of flame, a thumb on the piston
pulses LIFT OFF or ABORT.
My teleological aim the ovary moon,
will I ignite, jump, inject into the sky today
my sparkle of steel sperm?

. . . . Never so helpless, so choked with power.
Never so impotent, so important.
So naked, wrapped, equipped, and immobile,
cared for by 5000 nurses.
Let them siphon my urine to the nearest star.
Let it flare and spin like a Catherine.

. . . . T minus 10 . . . . The click of countdown stops.
My pram and mummycase, this trap's
tumescent tube's still locked to wet,
magnetic, unpredictable earth.
All my systems go, but oh,
an anger of the air won't let me go.
On the screen the blip is MISSION SCRUBBED.

. . . . Be dry my eye for nothing must leak
in here. If a tear forms, instruct the duct
to suck it back. Float, tadpole heart,
behind your slats of bone.
Keep your vibration steady, my switch of blood.
Eyeball in your nook of crepe
behind the ice shield of my window-face,
and ear within your muff of radio,
count taps against the hatch's darkening pane.
Out on the dome some innocent drops of rain.
A puny jolt of thunder. Lightning's golden sneer.

Note: On August 19, 1965, the launch of Gemini 5 from Pad 19 at Cape Canaveral was
"scrubbed" because of weather.

160

THE PEOPLE WALL*

Prodded by the smiles of handsome clerks,
they file into the narrow slits, and are filed,
500 every 20 minutes on 12 varicolored shelves.
All are carefully counted; all but their names are known.

It's been shown that 50 hips from the Midwest,
mainly female, with a random sprinkling of male and
juvenile, can fit into any given row, elbow to elbow
along the rail, heels hooked under the padded

8-inch-wide seat bar. Now the steep drawer
is filled, all the heads are filed, the racks closed
by the clerks at the ends of each aisle.
"Hello there!" calls the sartorially perfect head

clerk, let down on a circular podium to stand as if
in the air. He's propped like a stopped pendulum
in front of the wall of people all filed and smiling.
It's a colorful assortment of United States faces, good-

looking for the most part, fun-ready, circus-
expectant, and bright as a box of glazed marzipan.
"Hello there, all you people!" Twirling his
microphone cable like a lariat: "Do you know

where you're going on this Fair day? You're
going to be lifted . . . by mighty hydraulic arms . . .
straight up . . . 90 feet . . . up into The Egg!
In there you're going to learn how your mind works . . .

in color . . . on 15 separate screens . . . a show
that will show you how you all think! What do you think
of that? Now, just relax. Lean back. And no
smoking, please. Everybody comfortable? No need

*At the IBM pavilion, New York World's Fair, 1965.

to hold on to anything. Don't hold on to your hats,
or even your heads. Just lean back and get ready
for a pleasant ride backwards . . . There you go!
Up . . . up . . . up into the World of the Computers!''

Down on the ground, thousands of identical plastic
balls cascade through the maze of the Probability
Machine, repeatedly testing the Theory of the
Frequency of Errors. Clicking musically, they choose

their individual ways down, bouncing once before they
settle into the common heap. Each ball might
land in any one of 21 chutes, yet each chute fills
to about the same height each time the balls descend.

The magic curve completes itself. All balls
have fallen, and form a more or less symmetrical
black hill. A cheerful bell trills. The People Wall
rises. All heads, filed and smiling, are fed into The Egg.

STILL TURNING

Under a round roof the flying
horses, held by their heels to the disk of the
floor, move to spurts from a pillar of
    music, cranked from the past like grainy

    honey. Their ears are wood, their nostrils
painted red, their marble eyes
startled, distended with effort, their
    jaws carved grimaces of

    speed. Round and round go the flying
horses, backs arched in utmost
leaps, necks uptossed or stretched
    out, manes tangled by a wooden

    wind. As if lungs of wood inside their
chests pumped, their muscles
heave, and bunch beneath the colored
    traces. Round and round go the flying

    horses. Forked in the saddles are thrilled
children, with polished cheeks and fixed
eyes, who reach out in a stretch of
    ambition, leaning out from the turning

    pillar. They lean out to snatch the
rings, that are all of wood. But there's one of
brass. All feel lucky as, pass after
    pass, they stay fixed to the flying

    horses. The horses' reins and stirrups are
leather. Holes in the rumps spout actual
hair, that hangs to the heels that are held to the
    floor that wobbles around to the reedy

    tune. Their tails sweep out on a little
wind, that stirs the grass around the
disk, where the children sit and feel they
    fly, because real wind flies through their

hair. There is one motion and it is
round. There is one music, and its
sound issues from the fulcrum that
    repeats the grainy tune, forever

    wound in the flutings of wooden
ears. There is one luck (but it is
rare) that, if you catch, will grant
    release from the circle of the flying

    horses. But round and round on the fixed
horses, fashioned to look as if running
races, the children ride as if made of
    wood, till wrinkles carve their smiling

    faces, till blindness marbles all their
eyes. Round and round to the sagging
music, the children, all bewitched by their
    greeds, reach out to gather the wooden

    rings. And each ring makes a finger
stiff, as oil from the fulcrum blackens the
grass. Round and round go the flying
    hearses, carved and colored to look like steeds.

TO MAKE A PLAY

To make a play
is to make people,
to make people do
what you say;

to make real people
do and say
what you make;
to make people make

what you say real;
to make real
people make up
and do what you

make up. What you
make makes people
come and see
what people do

and say, and then
go away and do
what they see—
and see what

they do. Real
people do and say,
and you see and
make up people;

people come to see
what you do.
They see what *they*
do, and they

may go away undone.
You can make
people, or you
can unmake. You

can do or you
can undo. People
you make up make up
and make people;

people come to
see—to see
themselves real,
and they go away

and do what you
say—as if they
were made up,
and wore makeup.

To make a play
is to make
people; to make
people make

themselves; to
make people
make themselves
new. So real.

THE WATCH

When I
took my
watch to the watchfixer I
felt privileged but also pained to watch the operation. He
had long fingernails and a voluntary squint. He
fixed a magnifying cup over his
squint eye. He
undressed my
watch. I
watched him
split her
in three layers and lay her
middle—a quivering viscera—in a circle on a little plinth. He
shoved shirtsleeves up and leaned like an ogre over my
naked watch. With critical pincers he
poked and stirred. He
lifted out little private things with a magnet too tiny for me
to watch almost. "Watch out!" I
almost said. His
eye watched, enlarged, the secrets of my
watch, and I
watched anxiously. Because what if he
touched her
ticker too rough, and she
gave up the ghost out of pure fright? Or put her
things back backwards so she'd
run backwards after this? Or he
might lose a minuscule part, connected to her
exquisite heart, and mix her
up, instead of fix her.
And all the time,
all the time-
pieces on the walls, on the shelves, told the time,
told the time
in swishes and ticks,
swishes and ticks,

and seemed to be gloating, as they watched and told. I
felt faint, I
was about to lose my
breath—my
ticker going lickety-split—when watchfixer clipped her
three slices together with a gleam and two flicks of his
tools like chopsticks. He
spat out his
eye, lifted her
high, gave her
a twist, set her
hands right, and laid her
little face, quite as usual, in its place on my
wrist.

THE SECRET IN THE CAT

I took my cat apart
to see what made him purr.
Like an electric clock
or like the snore

of a warming kettle,
something fizzed and sizzled in him.
Was he a soft car,
the engine bubbling sound?

Was there a wire beneath his fur,
or humming throttle?
I undid his throat.
Within was no stir.

I opened up his chest
as though it were a door:
no whisk or rattle there.
I lifted off his skull:

no hiss or murmur.
I halved his little belly
but found no gear,
no cause for static.

So I replaced his lid,
laced his little gut.
His heart into his vest I slid
and buttoned up his throat.

His tail rose to a rod
and beckoned to the air.
Some voltage made him vibrate
warmer than before.

Whiskers and a tail:
perhaps they caught
some radar code
emitted as a pip, a dot-and-dash

of woolen sound.
My cat a kind of tuning fork?—
amplifier?—telegraph?—
doing secret signal work?

His eyes elliptic tubes:
there's a message in his stare.
I stroke him
but cannot find the dial.

WAKING FROM A NAP ON THE BEACH

Sounds like big
rashers of bacon frying.
I look up from where I'm lying
expecting to see stripes

red and white. My eyes drop shut,
stunned by the sun.
Now the foam is flame, the long
troughs charcoal, but

still it chuckles and sizzles, it
burns and burns, it never gets done.
The sea is that
fat.

RAIN AT WILDWOOD

The rain fell like grass growing
upside down in the dark,
at first thin shoots,
short, crisp, far apart,

but, roots in the clouds,
a thick mat grew
quick, loquacious, lachrymose blades
blunt on the tent top.

The grass beneath ticked,
trickled, tickled like rain
all night, inchwormed
under our ears,

its flat liquid tips slipping
east with the slope.
Various tin plates
and cups and a bucket filled

up outside,
played, plinked, plicked,
plopped till guttural.
The raccoon's prowl was almost

silent in the trash,
soggy everything but eggshells.
No owl called.
Waking at first light

the birds were blurred,
notes and dyes of jay and towhee
guaranteed to bleed.
And no bluing in the sky.

In the inverted V
of the tent flaps
muddy sheets of morning
slumped among the trunks,

but the pin oaks' veridian
dripping raggedy leaves
on the wood's floor released
tangy dews and ozones.

OCTOBER TEXTURES

The brushy and hairy,
tassely and slippery
willow, phragmite,
cattail, goldenrod.

The fluttery, whistley
water-dimpling divers,
waders, shovelers,
coots and rocking scaup.

Big blue, little green,
horned grebe, godwit,
bufflehead, ruddy,
marsh hawk, clapper rail.

Striated water
and striated feather.
The breast of the sunset.
The phalarope's breast.

CARDINAL IDEOGRAMS

0   A mouth. Can blow or breathe,
    be funnel, or Hello.

1   A grass blade or a cut.

2   A question seated. And a proud
    bird's neck.

3   Shallow mitten for two-fingered hand.

4   Three-cornered hut
    on one stilt. Sometimes built
    so the roof gapes.

5   A policeman. Polite.
    Wearing visored cap.

6   O unrolling,
    tape of ambiguous length
    on which is written the mystery
    of everything curly.

7   A step,
    detached from its stair.

8   The universe in diagram:
    A cosmic hourglass.
    (Note enigmatic shape,
    absence of any valve of origin,
    how end overlaps beginning.)
    Unknotted like a shoelace
    and whipped back and forth,
    can serve as a model of time.

9   Lorgnette for the right eye.
    In England or if you are Alice
    the stem is on the left.

10 A grass blade or a cut
    companioned by a mouth.
    Open? Open. Shut? Shut.

AFTER THE DENTIST

My left upper
lip and half

my nose is gone.
I drink my coffee

on the right from
a warped cup

whose left lip dips.
My cigarette's

thick as a finger.
Somebody else's.

I put lip-
stick on a cloth-

stuffed doll's
face that's

surprised when one
side smiles.

A YELLOW CIRCLE

A green
string
is fastened
to the earth,
at its apex
a yellow
circle
of silky
superimposed
spokes.
The sun
is its mother.

Later,
the string
is taller.
The circle
is white—
an aureole
of evanescent
hairs
the wind
makes breathe.

Later still,
it is altered;
the green
string
is thicker,
the white
circle
bald
on one side.
It is a half
circle
the wind lifts away.

from To Mix with Time

ABOVE THE ARNO

My room in Florence was the color of air.
Blue the stippled wall I woke to,
the tile floor white except where
shadowed by the washstand and my high
bed. Barefoot I'd go to the window to look
at the Arno. I'd open the broad shutters like a book,
and see the same scene. But each day's sky,
or night, dyed it a different light.

The lizard river might be green, or turbid gray,
or yellowish like the stucco palazzi
on the opposite quay.
Boys would be angling with long, lank
poles, sitting on the butts of them, dangling
legs from the paved bank;
they wore handkerchiefs, the corners knotted,
for caps against the strong

sun, and had their dogs along;
the dogs, brown-and-white spotted,
had to lie quiet. But I never saw anything
jerk the lines of the yellow poles.
The boys smoked a lot, and lazed in the sun.
Smaller ones dove and swam in the slow, snaking Arno
right under the sign that read: PERICOLO!
DIVIETO DI BAGNARSI.

Over Ponte Trinità, fiacres would go,
or a donkey-driven cart, among the auto
and popping scooter traffic. Freckled, gray,
blinkered horses trotted the red-and-black
carriages in which the richer tourists rode.
(A donkey looks like a bunny under its load,
with its wigwag ears and sweet expression;
the workman-driver flicks

a string-whip like a gadfly over it.)
I'd hear hoof-clops and heel-clicks
among hustling wheels on the bridge, that curved
like a violin's neck across the Arno.

It had two statues at each end—
white, graceful, a little funny.
One, a woman, had lost her head, but strode
forward holding her basket of fruit just the same.

You could see Giotto's Tower in my "book" and
the gold ball on top of Brunelleschi's Dome
and the clock with one hand
on the campanile of the Palazzo Vecchio,
and a blue slice of the Appenines the color of my room.
One day I slept all afternoon—
it was August and very hot—and didn't wake
until late at night,

or rather, early morning.
My mind was fresh—all was silent.
I crossed the white tiles, barefoot,
and opened the book of the shutters
to faint stars, to a full Arno,
starlight fingering the ripples. Gondola-slim
above the bridge, a new moon held a dim
circle of charcoal between its points.

Bats played in the greenish air,
their wing-joints
soft as moths' against the bone-gray palazzi where
not a window was alight,
the doorways dark as sockets.
Each of the four statues so white
and still,
rose somnambulistic from its hill

of stone, above the dusky slide
of the river. On my side,
a muscular, round-polled
man—naked behind—hugged a drape
against him, looking cold.
His partner, fat,
in short toga and hat
made of fruit, leaned a hand on a Horn

of Plenty. On the opposite bank, in torn

sweeping robes, a Signora
bore sheaves of wheat along her arm.
And, striding beside her with stately charm
in her broken flounces, the Headless One*
offered her wealthy basket, chin
up—though I had to imagine
chin, face, head, headdress, all.

Then a tall
tower began to tell F O U R,
and another with different timbre spelled it
a minute later. Another mentioned it for the third time
in harsh bronze and slow.
Still another, with delicate chime
countered and cantered it. By now the sky had turned
della Robbia blue, the Arno yellowed silver.

I stood between the covers of my book and heard
a donkey's particular heels,
like syllables of a clear, quick word,
echo over the Arno. Then came the scrape-clink
of milk cans lowered on cobbles. And with the moon still
there, but transparent, the sky began to fill
with downy clouds—pink
as the breasts of Botticelli's Venus—foretinting dawn.

*The head of Primavera was later found in October 1961 by workmen in the debris of the
Arno and restored to the statue.

NOTES MADE IN THE PIAZZA SAN MARCO

The wingèd lion on top of that column
(his paws have been patched, he appears to wear boots)
is bronze but has a white eye—
his tail sails out long . . . Could it help him fly?

On the other column St. Theodore
standing on an alligator,
he and it as white as salt,
wears an iron halo and an iron sword.

San Marco is crusty and curly with many crowns,
or is it a growth of golden thrones?
The five domes
covered, it looks like, with stiff crinkly parachute silk

have gold balls on twigs on turnip-tips,
sharp turrets in between with metal flags that cannot wave.
On all their perches statues gay and grave:
Erect somewhere among the towers a tall-necked woman

wearing an of-course-gold coronet
is helping a beast with baboon's head and lion's body to stand
on hindlegs. She's placing her hand
in his mouth . . . I wonder why.

In recesses of arches half in shade
are robed Venetians made
of red, blue, gold, green mosaics small as caramels,
fishermen encumbered by their robes launching a boat,

their faces all pricked out with those square
skin-colored pores . . .
Above them in a gold sky angels fly standing up.
About to step off the balcony

in the center of the main façade, four
horses exactly as big as horses but consciously more
handsome—gold running in rivulets
from their shoulders to under their bellies, their necks'

curt blade-shaped manes sloping like Roman helmets—
have a pair of heads front
and a pair to the side,
the lips tugged back into wide

loops. The bits are absent.
A pink and white checkered palace relatively plain
with a pleasant loggia halfway up
puts a rectangle out to the quay of the Grand Canal:

On one of its corners Adam and Eve look rueful, the Tree
between them—its low branches with leaves attached
happen to cover their genitals. Three
times hugged around the trunk, the serpent laughs.

There's often a rush of pigeons in the Piazza,
a leather scarf swept past your eyes
as if snatched from the ground,
when from the campanile great tongues let loose

and flog you, and flog you with gouts of iron sound.
The air must always burn deep blue here—
a velvet box for all that gold and white.
It turns thin and clear

toward the water. The Canal is a green vase lying down.
Gondolas knock their tethered necks on the quay:
Black, saddled with red, riderless, restless, they
are touching hips and shifting on the single-footing waves.

THE PANTHEON, ROME

Outside, pacing the sunken ramp around it
are many cats, scrofulous and starving.
The flutings of the columns of the portico
are bitten with age, their bases dark and urinous.
But the circle, the triangle, the square,
a solid geometric with caplike top,
squats here grimly eternal. Sixteen legs,
Corinthian, bear it up under the pronaos,
plain, harmonious. In gouges of the walls,
on accidental pediments of destroyed stone,
the fierce-eyed cats have taken occupation.

On a day of rain I pass into the interior,
through a door of bronze and leather—one slab
of which is agape. Inside is granite dusk
and dungeon cold—the round room no longer lined
with statues, the vault stripped of its gilt tiles.
Yet, there strike upon my chest the radii of grandeur.

The circle is large, the floor an immense coin
of porphyry and pavonazzetto; the dome of lead
is a strong belly; its rows of boxed blind windows
incise the entablature to the open disk at the top—
umbilical and only orifice for light.
That high lidless hole left for the sun to grin through
has not been closed since Agrippa.
Through it, now, rain rushes freely down
on the temple floor, to scour the dull colors
of the pattern that repeats, in giallo antico,
the eternal circle, the just square.

I walk around the tall, splattering column of rain
in the gloom. In a gray niche a dusty Christ
is stretched aloft—feet crossed and twisted,
head shadowed by iron thorns. On a shabby fresco
almost effaced, Mary with a stare of consternation
hears the Angel's smug pronouncement of her state.

Stooping, I discover Raphael's tomb, a bare stone box,
in a recess near the floor. Dust, thick as chalk,
powders the organ pipes, and the crude block
of the altar—installed when the Pantheon
was Christianized by Boniface in 609.
This temple stood before the Popes—
and Jove before Jesus—Minerva before the Virgin.
That empty arched embrasure remembers Bacchus laughing.
The rain that cannot ruin the floor,
the cats with demon eyes that crouch
around these walls, are fitting, are good.

ITALIAN SAMPLER

Lombardy, Tuscany, Umbria, Calabria.
A spear of leaves. A pear.
A clod-filled pasture dark as a bear.
Yellow blazes around a crown.

Lombardy, Tuscany, Umbria, Calabria.
Somber oxen. September flares.
Wind and silk, parchment and candles.
Slumberous, plushy, ponderous, elaborate.

A tree, a fruit, a pigment, an ornament.
Plumes, juices, bristles, crystals.
A mast. A horn. A bramble. A bride.
Lombardy, Tuscany, Umbria, Calabria.

DEATH INVITED

Death invited to break his horns
on the spread
cloth. To drop his head
on the dragged flag on the sand.
Death's hoofs slipping
in blood, and a band
of blood down the black side.
Death's tongue, curved in the open mouth
like a gray horn, dripping
blood. And
six colored agonies decking the summit
of his muscled pride.
Death invited to die.

The head
of death, with bewildered raging eye,
flagged down,
dragged down to the red
cloth on the sand.
Death invited to stand,
legs spread,
on the spot of the cape.
To buckle stubborn knees and lie
down in blood on the silken shape.
Beg blindness come to the sun-pierced eye.

The sword, sunk at the top of the shoulder's pride—
its hilt a silver cross—drawn forth now lets
hot radiant blood slide
from bubbling nostrils
through cloth to thirsty ground.

Yearning horns found
fleeing cloth and bloodless pillow,
substance none. Arrogant thighs,
that swiped and turned death by,
now, close as love, above lean lunging,
filling the pain-hot eye.

That stares till it turns to blood.
With the short knife dug
quick!
to the nape.
And the thick
neck drops on the spot of the cape.

Chains are drawn
round the horns, whose points are clean.
Trumpets shout.
New sand is thrown
where death's blood streamed.
Four stout,
jingling horses with gilded hoofs
tug death out.

Life is awarded ears and flowers.
Pelted with hats and shoes, and praise,
glittering life, in tight pink thighs,
swaggers around a rotunda of screams and *Olés*.

Death is dragged from the ring,
a clumsy hide,
a finished thing—
back to his pen.
The gate swings shut.

The gate swings wide.
Here comes trotting, snorting death
let loose again.

INSTEAD OF THE CAMARGUE

1

We hoped to find wild bulls and flamingos.
There were none there.
At Fos-sur-Mer
the wind whittled the gray sea to shingles

that, slanting, ran the reeds down.
Foils well-tempered,
they flew up again. Wind whimpered
over the fissured ramparts of the town.

We climbed to explore its church.
With the stone head of an elf
for tower, it sat on a stone shelf
high-hinged above the sea. This windy porch

held, as well, an ancient cemetery.
Marble-gabled steep *maisons,*
snug against *toutes les saisons,*
each housed a reliquary.

Tall, windowless sheds of tiny
width, in narrow yards—We wondered, were
the rag-robed bones standing within, for
they could not be lying. Shiny

nickel hearts, wreaths of mineral
flowers, fat sugar-white crosses,
and ceramic brooches bearing verses,
hung behind the ornate fences. No funeral

atmosphere. More like carnival.
For instance, rumps of rosy angels
fringed a tinted image of *Cher Papa.* Spangled
silver lilies blanketed a doll-

faced, smiling child
asleep in an ormolu pavilion; he hugged
a pink lamb that looked like candy. Tugged
by the wind (that failed

to fade or kill them) wax tulips, pansies,
peonies profused out of fix-footed urns.

On gilded grapes and vines
cherubs climbed in delicate frenzies

of carver's art: an arbor
of iron fruit and iron shade
stood over a dead
husband. Widow had built a harbor

durable as could be, for his soul's rest.
A populous white fondant and fuss of graves:
crosses shouldered each other, conclaves
of many identicals of the dying Christ

plastered on the chests
and foreheads of the huts—that stood for
bodies needing no roof and no floor—
a labyrinth, a jagged forest.

And where a flayed, white figurine
twined snakish on an occasional black
cross, or burned black on a gold one, the crack
in conformity frightened; the thin,

writhing form, sweating
in redundant chorused pain
against the dark grain,
was like a voodoo sign. Forgetting

to enter the *église*—outside
a Virgin with downcast eyes and upbent lips
held out the robust Child, her hand beneath His hips—
we wandered the macabre compound where He died

in every yard. And came to a miniature cathedral
with encrusted spires of colored tile,
even a little pointed window, playhouse style,
in the side, leaded and stained—a tetrahedral

tomb caked with carvings. On its gothic portal:
"Ici repose Maman aux bras de Dieu."
A tight embrace, we thought. And were it true,
her head must reach the belfry, she'd displace the altar.

At a neglected gate, two angels, kneeling,
clapped between broken

wings like violet mussel shells, raised stricken,
noseless faces to a peeling

shrine of metal, now corroded,
roofless. Beneath, a pair of marble beds,
moss-browned, sunk in weeds,
could not be read, the inscriptions faded.

But ovals of porcelain rimmed
with filigree forget-me-nots
and painted bleeding hearts,
their baked designs undimmed,

depended from the necks of the bitten
tombstones side by side.
We leaned to read
what graceful brush had written:

A Notre Fils	A Notre Fille
Il est passé	*Toi qui passa*
Comme un nuage	*Comme un nuage*
Comme un flot	*Emportant au Ciel*
Rapide en son cours	*Notre amour*
Et nos coeurs	*Nos coeurs garderont*
Gardent son image	*Ton image*
Toujours	*Toujours*

There were many "beds" most
neatly made, side by side and close together,
and unnumbered "houses" that the weather
would take long to unpost,

but the cracked stone
covers over these children (who had slept away
how many hundred birthdays in the clay?)
would soon be thrown

among the shards and slabs that leaned
in a corner of the wall—
the thick wall around this stone metropole,
that defended and screened

it from the living still at large. We
moved bemused in its gravel alleys, peeping

into curious stalls of the fête the dead were keeping
open above the sea.

Past a mélange of flamboyant and somber things,
butterflies (of pressed paper), hectic flowers,
black-wrapped stars and harps, and wire
hourglasses with wings,

we came to the gate's gap, where the wind squalled
and sun smote the rock stair
going down. In a corner there,
by sharp dark cypress enwalled,

was hidden a tomb square and plain:
A lean and beautiful lion
couched on the lid—rivet-eyed scion
and emblem of France—his mane

a cowl of grim, roughened stone
black from the rains—one paw bent
on the lock of the grave, but negligent,
upturned, the other—as all lions are known

to lie—guardianship
alerting his nostrils, his chest raised.
His cool, secret smile grazed
us, and the ancient patience at his lip.

Chiseled below, on his pedestal:
"*Ici Repose Le Gendarme Pierre
Pecot, Tué Par Un Braconnier,
1752*"—within a wreath of laurel.

2

We saw no wild bulls or flamingos that day.
To reach the Camargue, we agreed
we would need
to have gone by another way—

north, then west around the delta of the Rhône.
Descending to the flats, we drove the straight
road between sea and slate
marsh, where rice is grown.

We saw shorebirds wade
near the floating corks

of fishermen's nets. Not Moroccan storks
or Egyptian ibises, as the guidebook had said,

but ordinary checkered sanderlings, and a lone heron.
We turned back through the red hills, *terres rougeâtres,* where,
above the Etang de Berre,
the incessant mistral blows—and came to an environ

of Van Gogh. Great umber faces
headdressed in flames—round
ruffed faces, Indian and profound,
on totem stalks thick as maces—

stared: a company of giant
sunflowers. Like eclipses of the sun,
their plate-heads, almost black, spun
within the yellow aureoles; only the pliant

broad leaves sagged on their spikes in the heat.
East of the divide,
nearing Aix, on the cooler side,
the tranquil valley fell away. Cut wheat

stood in blond hives on the slant
hills. We passed fields of smoky lavender, ditches
full of poppies flaring like lit matches
and young grapevines planted

in ruled brown earth. The road became a funnel: arching
sycamores, their pinto-spotted trunks tan
and gray, with painted white belts, ran
by the car, the low sun torching

through. Beyond the opening of that shade-
striped bower,
Cézanne's mountain, Saint-Victoire,
unfolded its blue knife-blade

on the sky. Against the rind
of evening, its acute shape
blunted, enlarging on the landscape.
We circled fruit and olive orchards, poplar-lined,

and watched how shadows massed
in the concaves of that head,
the impenetrable Pharaoh-face that baffled
all the painters of Provence, until Cézanne in his last

attempt, defined it with simple
brush as tender vapor, a mirage:
"Au lieu de se tasser, immense et sauvage,
elle respire et participe toute bleutée de l'air ample."

3

We never found the blackfaced bulls
and rouge flamingos, except on
postcards . . . We bought one
showing three skulls,

a rosary, and a knapsack
that are among Cézanne's effects
in his studio at Aix,
and twirling the rack

with other tourists on Cours Mirabeau,
also bought views of the exotic Camargue—the small
gray horses in tall
grass, the high-horned, stubborn *taureaux*—

and of gypsies at Fos-sur-Mer.
"La Méditerranée a une couleur comme les maquereaux,"
said the back of a card, quoting Van Gogh,
who used to walk there

"sur la plage déserte." We sat
sipping coffee in the oasis
of Aix, the fountain's breath in our faces,
remembering that

a sign by the cemetary gate had said: "It is forbidden
to photograph the houses of the dead."
We could not buy our lion, spread
dark and lean upon a card. We're glad he's hidden.

FOUNTAINS OF AIX

Beards of water
some of them have.
Others are blowing whistles of water.
Faces astonished that constant water
jumps from their mouths.
Jaws of lions are snarling water
through green teeth over chins of moss.
Dolphins toss jets of water
from open snouts
to an upper theatre of water.
Children are riding swans and water
coils from the S-shaped necks and spills
in flat foils from pincered bills.
A solemn curly-headed bull
puts out a swollen tongue of water.
Cupids naked are making water
into a font that never is full.
A goddess is driving a chariot through water.
Her reins and whips are tight white water.
Bronze hoofs of horses wrangle with water.
Marble faces half hidden in leaves.
Faces whose hair is leaves and grapes
of stone are peering from living leaves.
Faces with mossy lips unlocked
always uttering water,
water
wearing their features blank
their ears deaf, their eyes mad
or patient or blind or astonished at water
always uttered out of their mouths.

WHILE SITTING IN THE TUILERIES AND FACING
THE SLANTING SUN

There is the	Line
There is the	Circle
the bending	Line
the expanding	Circle
There is the moving	Line
but the still	Circle
but the enlarging	Circle
the lengthening	Line
The	Crack
and the	Particle
the deepening	Crack
the doubling redoubling	Particle
the	Splitting
and	Resplitting
then the	Multiple
the opening	Closing
then the closure	Opening
There is a	Swaddled Thing
There is a	*Swaddled Thing*
There is a	Rocking Box
There is a	*Covered Box*
The	Unwrapping
the	Ripening
Then the	Loosening
the	Spoiling
The	Stiffening
then the	Wrapping
The	Softening
but the long long	Drying
The	Wrapping
the	Wrapping
the	Straightening

and	Wrapping
The rigid	Rolling
the gilded	Scrolling
The	Wrapping
and	Wrapping
and careful	Rewrapping
The	Thinning
and	Drying
but the	Wrapping
and	Fattening
There is the worm	Coiled
and the straw	Straightened
There is the	Plank
and the glaucous	Bundle
the paper	Skull
and the charred	Hair
the linen	Lip
and the leather	Eyelid
There is a	Person
of flesh that is *a rocking*	*Box*
There is a	Box
of wood that is a *painted*	*Person*

NOTE FROM A DIARY: I sat an hour on a bench in the Tuileries by a frozen flower bed. The sunrays striking between my lashes made gilt slits, black dots. I felt rolled up in a spool of light——face warm, feet numb——a kind of mesmerization . . . And remembered Giotto's fresco *Birth of the Virgin* in a cloister in Florence: the "Mother of God" was a swaddled infant held upright, like a board or plaque, by her nurse——the halo a gilt bonnet around the tiny head with its fugitive eyes . . . And I remembered a mummy in the Vatican Museum in Rome: in her sarcophagus shaped and painted like herself, an Egyptian girl 2000 years old lay unwrapped to the waist, and with hands and feet bare——her nails, hair, lips and eyelids frangible as tobacco leaf, but intact. Still exquisite, merely dried and darkened, was her youth.

A HURRICANE AT SEA

Slowly a floor rises, almost becomes a wall.
Gently a ceiling slips down, nearly becomes a floor.
A floor with spots that stretch, as on a breathing
animal's hide. It rises again with a soft lurch.

The floor tilts, is curved, appears to be racing north
with a pattern of dents and dips
over slashes of dark. Now there are white lips,
widening on the wall

that stands up suddenly. The ceiling is all
rumpled, snarled, like a wet animal's fur.
The floor hardens, humps up like rock,
the side of a hill too slant to walk.

White teeth are bared where lazy lips swam.
The ceiling is the lid of a box about to slam.
Is this a real floor I walk? It's an angry spine
that shoots up over a chasm of seething

milk—cold, churned, shoving the stern around.
There's the groaning sound
of a cauldron about to buckle, maybe break.
A blizzard of glass and lace

shivers over this dodging box.
It glides up the next high hissing alp—halts
on top. But the top turns hollow while the hollow spins.
I run down a slope and feel like twins,

one leg northeast, one west.
The planks pitch leeward, level an instant, then
rear back to a flat, stunned rest.
It's frightening, that vacant moment. I feel

the Floor beneath the floor reel,
while a thickening wilderness is shunted aft, under.
I'm in a bottle becalmed, but a mountain bloats
ahead, ready to thunder

on it. The floor is rushed into the pit.
Maybe there's no bottom to it.
I'm buried in a quarry, locked in a bucking
room—or bottle, or box—near cracking,

that's knocked about in a black,
enormous, heavy, quaking Room.
Is there a bottom to it? I'm glad not to have to know.
Boulders, canyon-high, smash down on the prow,

are shattered to snow, and shouldered off somehow.
Tossed out again on top. Topside bounced
like a top, to scoot the bumpy floor . . .
Out there, it's slicked to a plane almost, already,

though chopped with white to the far baseboard.
The ceiling is placing
itself right, getting steadier,
licking itself smooth. The keel

takes the next swollen hills along their backs—
like a little dog gripped
to a galloping horse—slipping
once in a while, but staying on.

SNOW IN NEW YORK

It snowed in New York. I walked on Fifth
Avenue and saw the orange snowplow cut the drifts
with rotary sickles, suck up celestial clods into its turning neck,
a big flue that spewed them into a garbage truck.
This gift from the Alps was good for nothing, though scarcely gray.
The bright apparatus, with hungry noise,
crumbled and mauled the new hills. Convoys
of dump-cars hauled them away.

I went to Riker's to blow my nose
in a napkin and drink coffee for its steam. Two rows
of belts came and went from the kitchen, modeling scrambled
eggs, corn muffins, bleeding triangles of pie.
Tubs of dirty dishes slid by.
Outside the fogged window black bulking people stumbled
cursing the good-for-nothing whiteness. I thought
of Rilke, having read how he wrote

to Princess Marie von Thurn und Taxis, saying: "The idea haunts me—
it keeps on calling—I must make a poem for Nijinski
that could be, so to say, swallowed and then danced." Printed
as on the page, in its
remembered place in the paragraph, that odd name with three dots
over the *iji,* appeared—as I squinted
through the moist window past the traveling
dishes—against the snow. There unraveled

from a file in my mind a magic notion
I, too, used to play with: from chosen words a potion
could be wrung; pickings of them, eaten, could make you fly, walk
on water, be somebody else, do or undo anything, go back
or forward on belts of time. But then I thought:
Snow in New York is like poetry, or clothes made of roses.
Who needs it, what can you build with snow, who can you feed? Hoses
were coming to whip back to water, wash to the sewers the nuisance-freight.

RIDING THE "A"

I ride
the "A" train
and feel
like a ball-
bearing in a roller skate.
I have on a gray
rain-
coat. The hollow
of the car
is gray.
My face
a negative in the slate
window,
I sit
in a lit
corridor that races
through a dark
one. Strok-
ing steel,
what a smooth rasp—it feels
like the newest of knives
slicing
along
a long
black crusty loaf
from West 4th to 168th.
Wheels
and rails
in their prime
collide,
make love in a glide
of slickness
and friction.
It is an elation
I wish to pro-
long.
The station
is reached
too soon.

A FIXTURE

Women women women women
in a department store
with hats on (hats in *it*)
and shoes on (shoes in *it*)
dresses coats gloves on (and *in*
all the departments)

In the lobby (in a niche)
between two glass revolving doors
sluff sluff sluff sluff
(rubber bottoms of whirling doors)
flick flick click click
(women in women out) sits a nun

In the mid-whirl (a station)
white black wooden (a fixture)
holding a wooden cup she sits
between the glitter of double doors
hexagonal glasses glittering
over glassy fixed eyes

A garter snake of black
beads (wooden?) catching light
crawling (clicking) crawling
(clicking) up her draped
fixed short carved
black knees (thighs)

Her white hat (hood) a head cover
her shoes short black
flat (foot covers)
her dress a black curtain (cape)
over a longer curtain shape
she is the best dressed

THE CONTRAPTION

Going up is pleasant. It tips your chin,
    and you feel tall and free
as if in control of, and standing in,
    a chariot, hands feeling the frisky

reins. But, doubled in your seat,
    knuckled to the fun-car's handrails,
you mount baby-buggied, cleat by cleat,
    to that humped apogee your entrails

aren't ready for. Wind in your
    ears, clouds in your eyes, it's easy
to define the prophetic jelly at your core
    as joy. The landscape of amusement goes queasy

only when the gilded buckboard juts straight out
    over undippered air. A jaw of horror will spill
        you? Not yet. The route
becomes a roaring trough for the next hill

hairpinning higher. You wish you had
    the chance to count how many ups,
        downs and switchbacks the mad
rattler, rearing its steel hoops, has. The divan hiccups

over a straightaway now, at mild speed.
Then you look: Jolly carousel and Ferris wheel, far
years beneath, are cruel gears you can be emptied
    into over the side of the hellish sled. Star-

beaded sky! (It feels better to look higher.) How
    did the morning, the whole blue-and-white day
go by in what seems one swoop? You vow
    to examine the contraption and its fairway,

measure the system of gruesome twists,
the queer dimensions, if ever you get down. Going

down is a dull road. Your fists
loosen, pretend no longer, knowing

they grip no stick of purpose. The final chutes are
unspectacular, slower repetitions of past
excitements. A used and vulgar car
shovels you home in a puzzling gloom. The vast

agitation faded in your bowels, you think
that from the ground you'll trace the rim
your coaster sped and crawled, the sink
and rise, the reason for its shape. Grim

darkness now. The ride
is complete. You are positioned for discovery, but,
your senses gone, you can't see the upper arching works. Wide
silence. Midnight. The carnival is shut.

AT THE MUSEUM OF MODERN ART

At the Museum of Modern Art you can sit in the lobby
on the foam-rubber couch; you can rest and smoke,
and view whatever the revolving doors express.
You don't have to go into the galleries at all.

In this arena the exhibits are free and have all
the surprises of art—besides something extra:
sensory restlessness, the play of alternation,
expectation in an incessant spray

thrown from heads, hands, the tendons of ankles.
The shifts and strollings of feet
engender compositions on the shining tiles,
and glide together and pose gambits,

gestures of design, that scatter, rearrange,
trickle into lines, and turn clicking through a wicket
into rooms where caged colors blotch the walls.
You don't have to go to the movie downstairs

to sit on red plush in the snow and fog
of old-fashioned silence. You can see contemporary
Garbos and Chaplins go by right here.
And there's a mesmeric experimental film

constantly reflected on the flat side of the wide
steel-plate pillar opposite the crenellated window.
Non-objective taxis surging west, on Fifty-third,
liquefy in slippery yellows, dusky crimsons,

pearly mauves—an accelerated sunset, a roiled
surf, or cloud-curls undulating—their tubular ribbons
elongations of the coils of light itself
(engine of color) and motion (motor of form).

DISTANCE AND A CERTAIN LIGHT

Distance
and a certain light
makes anything artistic—
it doesn't matter what.

From an airplane, all
that rigid splatter of the Bronx
becomes organic, logical
as web or beehive. Chunks

of decayed cars in junkyards,
garbage scows (nimble roaches
on the Harlem), herds of stalled
manure-yellow boxes on twisting reaches

of rails, are punched clean and sharp
as ingots in the ignition of the sun.
Rubbish becomes engaging shape—
you only have to get a bead on it,

the right light filling the corridor
of your view—a gob of spit
under a microscope, fastidious
in structure as a crystal. No contortion

without intention, and nothing ugly.
In any random, sprawling, decomposing thing
is the charming string
of its history—and what it will be next.

PIGEON WOMAN

Slate, or dirty-marble-colored,
or rusty-iron-colored, the pigeons
on the flagstones in front of the
Public Library make a sharp lake

into which the pigeon woman wades
at exactly 1:30. She wears a
plastic pink raincoat with a round
collar (looking like a little

girl) and flat gym shoes,
her hair square-cut, orange.
Wide-apart feet carefully enter
the spinning, crooning waves

(as if she'd just learned how
to walk, each step conscious,
an accomplishment); blue knots in the
calves of her bare legs (uglied marble),

age in angled cords of jaw
and neck, her pimento-colored hair,
hanging in thin tassels, is gray
around a balding crown.

The day-old bread drops down
from her veined hand dipping out
of a paper sack. Choppy, shadowy ripples,
the pigeons strike around her legs.

Sack empty, she squats and seems to rinse
her hands in them—the rainy greens and
oily purples of their necks. Almost
they let her wet her thirsty fingertips—

but drain away in an untouchable tide.
A make-believe trade

she has come to, in her lostness
or illness or age—to treat the motley

city pigeons at 1:30 every day, in all
weathers. It is for them she colors
her own feathers. Ruddy-footed
on the lime-stained paving,

purling to meet her when she comes,
they are a lake of love. Retreating
from her hands as soon as empty,
they are the flints of love.

CAT & THE WEATHER

Cat takes a look at the weather.
Snow.
Puts a paw on the sill.
His perch is piled, is a pillow.

Shape of his pad appears.
Will it dig? No.
Not like sand.
Like his fur almost.

But licked, not liked.
Too cold.
Insects are flying, fainting down.
He'll try

to bat one against the pane.
They have no body and no buzz.
And now his feet are wet;
it's a puzzle.

Shakes each leg,
then shakes his skin
to get the white flies off.
Looks for his tail,

tells it to come on in
by the radiator.
World's turned queer
somehow. All white,

no smell. Well, here
inside it's still familiar.
He'll go to sleep until
it puts itself right.

A COUPLE

A bee
rolls
in the yellow
rose.
Does she
invite his hairy
rub?
He scrubs
himself
in her creamy
folds.
A bullet soft imposes
her spiral and, spinning, burrows
to her dewy
shadows.
The gold
grooves almost
match
the yellow
bowl.
Does his touch
please
or scratch?
When he's
done
his honey-
thieving
at her matrix,
whirs free
leaving,
she
closes,
still
tall, chill,
unrumpled on her stem.

SOUTHBOUND ON THE FREEWAY

A tourist came in from Orbitville,
parked in the air, and said:

The creatures of this star
are made of metal and glass.

Through the transparent parts
you can see their guts.

Their feet are round and roll
on diagrams—or long

measuring tapes—dark
with white lines.

They have four eyes.
The two in the back are red.

Sometimes you can see a five-eyed
one, with a red eye turning

on the top of his head.
He must be special—

the others respect him,
and go slow,

when he passes, winding
among them from behind.

They all hiss as they glide,
like inches, down the marked

tapes. Those soft shapes,
shadowy inside

the hard bodies—are they
their guts or their brains?

THE WOODS AT NIGHT

The binocular owl,
fastened to a limb
like a lantern
all night long,

sees where all
the other birds sleep:
towhee under leaves,
titmouse deep

in a twighouse,
sapsucker gripped
to a knothole lip,
redwing in the reeds,

swallow in the willow,
flicker in the oak—
but cannot see poor
whippoorwill

under the hill
in deadbrush nest,
who's awake, too—
with stricken eye

flayed by the moon
her brindled breast
repeats, repeats, repeats its plea
for cruelty.

LIVING TENDERLY

My body a rounded stone
with a pattern of smooth seams.
My head a short snake,
retractive, projective.
My legs come out of their sleeves
or shrink within,
and so does my chin.
My eyelids are quick clamps.

My back is my roof.
I am always at home.
I travel where my house walks.
It is a smooth stone.
It floats within the lake,
or rests in the dust.
My flesh lives tenderly
inside its bone.

THE EXCHANGE

Now, my body flat, the ground
breathes. I'll be the grass.

Populous and mixed is mind.
Earth, take thought. My mouth, be moss.

Field, go walking. I, a disk,
will look down with seeming eye.

I will be time, and study to be evening.
You, world, be clock.

I will stand, a tree, here,
never to know another spot.

Wind, be motion. Birds, be passion.
Water, invite me to your bed.

THE UNIVERSE

What
          is it about,
     the universe,
     the universe about us stretching out?
We, within our brains,
          within it,
               think

we must unspin
the laws that spin it.
          We think *why*
     because we think
     because.
     Because we think,
          we think
               the universe about us.

But does it think,
          the universe?
               Then what about?
                    About us?
          If not,
must there be cause
          in the universe?
     Must it have laws?
               And what
     if the universe
               is not about us?
          Then what?
          What
               is it about?
          And what
               about *us?*

GOD

They said there was a Thing
that could not Change
They could not Find
it so they Named
it God
They had to Search
so then it must be There
It had a Name
It must exist Somewhere
The Name
was God
the Thing
that could not Change
They could not Find
it What is Lost
is God
They had to Search
for what could not be Found
What can't be Found
is Changeless
It is God
The Name
is clue The Thing
is Lost
Somewhere
They Found
the Name
The Name
is Changeless
God

THE WISH TO ESCAPE INTO INNER SPACE

All is too open:
all expands, explodes
and scampers out and speeds apart.
What was a ball, and solid, now balloons,
the outline thin, the core weightless.

What was full, and held to a pole centripetal,
what gathered, while it spun, coherent mass,
seized light, shape, ordered time and motion,
worked upon itself its own proportion:
to be round, smooth in its orbit,
beautifully closed—

spurts loose, erratic, widens,
torn from its core,
feels itself emptied, floats detached . . .
is dragged through galactic vapors:
the cold pain of unwanted growth.

LANDING ON THE MOON

When in the mask of night there shone that cut,
we were riddled. A probe reached down
and stroked some nerve in us,
as if the glint from a wizard's eye, of silver,
slanted out of the mask of the unknown—
pit of riddles, the scratch-marked sky.

When, albino bowl on cloth of jet,
it spilled its virile rays,
our eyes enlarged, our blood reared with the waves.
We craved its secret, but unreachable
it held away from us, chilly and frail.
Distance kept it magnate. Enigma made it white.

When we learned to read it with our rod,
reflected light revealed
a lead mirror, a bruised shield
seamed with scars and shadow-soiled.
A half-faced sycophant, its glitter borrowed,
rode around our throne.

On the moon there shines earth light
as moonlight shines upon the earth . . .
If on its obsidian we set our weightless foot,
and sniff no wind, and lick no rain
and feel no gauze between us and the Fire,
will we trot its grassless skull, sick for the homelike shade?

Naked to the earth-beam we will be,
who have arrived to map an apparition,
who walk upon the forehead of a myth.
Can flesh rub with symbol? If our ball
be iron, and not light, our earliest wish
eclipses. Dare we land upon a dream?

OUT OF MY HEAD

```
                  If I could get
        out    of my
       head    and
       into    the
      world.
                  What am I saying?
        Out    of my
      head?
                  Isn't my
       head
         in    the
      world?
         In    it I'm
         in    it, a
      round
      place
         in    a bigger
      round
      place
   someplace.
                  Seems like the
     center.
                  Every
       head
         in    there's a
     center,   it
      thinks.
                  It
      thinks!
                  O.K., let's say I'm
        out    and
         in    the
      round    free
      world:
       Back    there's the tight aluminum sphere
                  I jumped
        out    of, slammed the door like an icebox.
                  A clean landscape
```

around me, an inch or two of "snow"—
        rock-dust from those
peaks
    in the distance. No colder here,
        even if it is wider. Very few things
around —just the
peaks. It'll take weeks to reach them.
        Of course I came here in my
head.
        I'll be taking it
back.
        The idea is to make a vehicle
    out of it.

THE PRIMITIVE

I walk a path that a mountain crosses.
I am walking toward the mountain.
I have been making the path, I suppose.
Its track is behind me. I see how it goes
ahead of me also. Perhaps I make it with my eyes.
    Then have I made the mountain also?
More likely the mountain makes itself,
and lets me walk here. Or it lets the path
come upon it. And whatever may be
on the path may approach . . . Why not?
    Or perhaps, thrown out by the mountain once,
like a stone I fell here. Or I fell
in the path farther back, where it already lay.
And then started on my way,
as now, toward the mountain.
    The thing is, I cannot see over the mountain.
It is there, a gradual great rise of the ground.

As I walk, I am crossing it really, already:
the path is rising ever so gently.
But there is the peak. Do I want to go *over* the mountain?

    I see I have come quite far already.
It is strange to look back . . . as if down a thread
with no knot! Before me the path is almost level,
and narrow. But higher, ahead
on the mountain's wedge, it widens. That is strange.
    What would I prefer, then? To stay here,
midway, facing the mountain? To stop,
and not look up or down? Or to drop
back, downwards? I ask myself such things, *while walking!*
—and smile to myself. *Forward, forward is the only choice.*

    But am I sure of this? What if, for instance,
I do make the path with my eyes?
And since it is on the mountain,
I am making the mountain?
There is no one else on this path, after all.
    All the others—although in some way
it is also theirs—this mountain—
their paths make it a separate mountain.
Yet it is mine, in some same parallel way
as I am all the others. I notice this sometimes.
    They are all around me, beside me, walking.
Or within me, when I remember them.
So that they are myself.
So then I am all alone on this mountain?
It must be that I make it. With my eyes?

    I am walking, and talking to myself as I walk—up—
the mountain. I will come to the summit at last.
There are no separate ways about that . . .
Which ought to be a good thing. Except that,
will I know when I reach the peak?
    Will I see *the other side?* I can't "see"
what it may be like—the other side. Except
as being like *this* side . . . No, no,
that would be too foolish! And then,
there is the omen . . . that I shall go blind.

It is said that this happens
before reaching the peak, so that no one may know
just when he is crossing the mountain.
Then have my eyes, that made this path, that make
this mountain, made this fate for themselves?

Oh, eyes, turn and look at me,
instead of always ahead or behind! No, no, no,
such a thing is insane! Mountain, again
you have thrown me back, and down, like a stone!
You are the One! I am yours.
There is nothing I can know but you.
And I can never know you. Yet we are each other,
are we not? As a pebble is a fraction of the rock
it came from? I must know you, as I know myself.
Exactly that. *But need you know me?*
Am I not rolling up to you, mountain, as I walk?
Was I "thrown away" upon your self-forgotten body,
and are you now pulling me into your great head again?
Will you let me, finally, see your other side?
Surely someone may see it, sometime?
What if I, steadfastly, determine
to reach your peak, *without going blind?*
If you can throw me from yourself,
you can take me as quickly up.
Or I will hurry to climb, faithfully, by myself.
I PROMISE
NEVER
TO TAKE MY EYES
FROM YOUR PEAK.
Mountain, give me a sign!

No . . . I think, rather, that you do not care.
Perhaps it is a small nobility to think this way . . .
Can pebbles expect a summit?
Enough that we have "eyes"—for a time.
Strange enough. *I cannot understand it.*

218

HOW TO BE OLD

It is easy to be young. (Everybody is,
at first.) It is not easy
to be old. It takes time.
Youth is given; age is achieved.
One must work a magic to mix with time
in order to become old.

Youth is given. One must put it away
like a doll in a closet,
take it out and play with it only
on holidays. One must have many dresses
and dress the doll impeccably
(but not to show the doll, to keep it hidden).

It is necessary to adore the doll,
to remember it in the dark on the ordinary
days, and every day congratulate
one's aging face in the mirror.

In time one will be very old.
In time, one's life will be accomplished.
And in time, in time, the doll—
like new, though ancient—may be found.

NIGHT PRACTICE

I
will
remember
with my breath
to make a mountain,
with my sucked-in breath
a valley, with my pushed-out
breath a mountain. I will make
a valley wider than the whisper, I
will make a higher mountain than the cry;
will with my will breathe a mountain, I will
with my will breathe a valley. I will push out
a mountain, suck in a valley, deeper than the shout
YOU MUST DIE, harder, heavier, sharper a mountain than
the truth YOU MUST DIE. I will remember. My breath will
make a mountain. My will will remember to will. I, suck-
ing, pushing, I will breathe a valley, I will breathe a mountain.

LET US PREPARE

to get beyond the organic
for surely there is something else
to which it is an impediment an opaque pod
What if it is sight that blinds
hearing that deafens
touch that makes us numb?
What if trussed in a jacket of blood
to a rack of bone we smother
in the dungeon of our lungs?
Today we are in our brain
a laboratory
Must we be here
tomorrow?
Are there not
pinnacles
on which to stand
cleanly
without a head?
Between the belly
of the sun and the belly
of the world
must we bounce forever
magnetized generations of the circle?
Let us eat nothing but darkness
refuse our stale orbit
and walk only in sleep
There to descry a crack in the future
and work to widen it
Let us prepare to bare ourselves outside the gibbet-hood
of the world
without excuse of flesh or apology of blood

THE SURFACE

First I saw the surface,
then I saw it flow,
then I saw the underneath.

In gradual light below
I saw a kind of room,
the ceiling was a veil,
a shape swam there
slow, opaque and pale.

I saw enter by a shifting corridor
other blunt bodies
that sank toward the floor.

I tried to follow deeper
with my avid eye.
Something changed the focus:
I saw the sky,
a glass between inverted trees . . .

Then I saw my face.
I looked until a cloud
flowed over that place.

Now I saw the surface
broad to its rim,
here gleaming, there opaque,
far out, flat and dim.

Then I saw it was an Eye:
I saw the Wink that slid
from underneath the surface
before it closed its lid.

from A Cage of Spines

AT
BREAKFAST

Not quite
spherical
White
Oddly closed
and without a lid

A smooth miracle
here in my hand
Has it slid
from my sleeve?

The shape
of this box
keels me oval
Heels feel
its bottom
Nape knocks
its top

Seated
like a foetus
I look for
the dream-seam

What's inside?
A sun?
Off with its head
though it hasn't any
or is all head no body
a
One

Neatly
the knife scalps it
I scoop out
the braincap
soft
sweetly shuddering
Mooncream
this could be
Spoon
laps the larger
crescent
loosens a gilded
nucleus
from warm pap
A lyrical food

Opened
a seamless miracle
Ate a sun-germ
Good

BY MORNING

Some for everyone
   plenty

   and more coming

Fresh   dainty   airily arriving
   everywhere at once

Transparent at first
   each faint slice
   slow   soundlessly tumbling

    then quickly thickly a gracious fleece
    will spread like youth   like wheat
    over the city

Each building will be   a hill
   all sharps made round

    dark worn noisy narrows made still
    wide   flat   clean   spaces

Streets will be   fields
   cars be   fumbling sheep

A deep bright harvest will be seeded
   in a night

By morning we'll be   children
   feeding on manna

    a new loaf on every doorsill

HYPNOTIST

His lair framed beneath the clock
a red-haired beast hypnotic in the room
glazes our eyes draws us close
with delicious snarls and flickers of his claws
We stir our teacups and our wishes feast
on his cruelty

Throw the Christian chairs to him
a wild child in us cries
Or let us be Daniel bared
to that seething maze his mane
Loops of his fur graze the sill
where the clock's face looks scared

Comfort-ensnared and languorous
our unused daring roused resembles him
fettered on the hearth's stage
behind the iron dogs
He's the red locks of the sun
brought home to a cage

Hunched before his flaring shape
we stir our teacups
We wish he would escape
and loosen in ourselves the terrible
But only his reflection pounces
on the parquet and the stair

WAS WORM

Was worm
swaddled in white

Now tiny queen
in sequin coat
peacockbright
drinks the wind
and feeds
on sweat of the leaves

Is little chinks
of mosaic floating
or a scatter
of colored beads

Alighting pokes
with her new black wire
the saffron yokes

On silent hinges
openfolds her wings'
applauding hands

Weaned
from coddling white
to lakedeep air
to blue and green

Is queen

AN EXTREMITY

Roused from napping in my lap
this nimble animal or five-legged star
parts its limbs sprat-wide
See where they glide to focus at their base as spokes of a harp
Blunt and fat the first
sharp-tipped tapping the next
the third authentic and the fourth shy
the least a runt begs pardon for his stature
Why they're separate beasts I see
and not one beast with legs

Or a family of dolls
you could dress the tallest as a boy
already his sister wears a silver belt
that's a toy-baby by her curled if you put a bonnet on it
Here's agile-joint the pointed the smart wife
Square-head short and papa-perfect
sits apart in dignity a wart at knuckle

Turned over open inner skin is vellum
Here's a map
five islands spread from the mainland in the fist
Seen flat it's a plain
forked rivers thread to the wrist
or call them roads the rosy pattern sprawled in an M
Forests are stitched with prick-hatched pinetree criss-marks
Whorled lines are ploughed land
and ending each pentacle beach are U-bands of sea-rippled sand

Left one looked at
right one writes Star Harp Beast Family of Five
Map laid live in my lap
Clapped together the two arrive are stated
the poem made extremities mated

R.F. AT BREAD LOAF
HIS HAND AGAINST A TREE

His hand on the saw
    ed off should
    er of a tree
Companions he and the cross
    grained bark
    crusted fellow from whose stub
    born t hickness limb
    er switches lean
    and wag young leaves
Lines in that hand
    whorls in that tree re
    cord a brother's chronic
    le the stoic accrual of s
    elfhood from the c ore out
Flat of his palm and flat
    of the cut fork meet fit
    tingly
Lots of trees in the fo
    rest but this one's an O
    a K that's plan
    ted hims elf and nob
    oddy has k nots of that hand
    some polish or the knarl
    edge of ear th or the obs
    tiny ate servation his blueyes
    make or the tr easures his sent
    ient t humb les find
His sig nature's on the he art
    of his time
Snowcrop on rude dy square b
    locked f orehead
    on summer's dreamhead
Snowrims over w him sey t wink
    led blueyes
And veined in autumn g love
    that ax and ax
    iom h ardent hand
Oh may it feel many sp rings
    widening warm hone y ed
    g lad as the c limb of youth

FRONTISPIECE

In this book I see your face and in your face
your eyes holding the world and all else besides
like a cat's pupils rayed and wide
to what is before them and what more alive
ticks in the shadows flickers in the waves

Your hair in a slow stream curves
from your listening brow
to your ear shaped like a sea-thing found
in that water-haunted house where murmurs
your chaste-fierce name   The vow

that corners your mouth
compelled you to that deep between words and acts
where they cross as sand with salt
There spills the layered light
your sockets lips and nostrils drank

before they sank
On stages of the sea the years tall
tableaus build   The lighthouse you commanded
the room the oak and mutable Orlando
reoccur as the sea's pages to land's mind   The wall

the steep and empty slate
your cane indented until you laid it as a mark
above where the tide would darken
in weed and shell is written how you were sane
when walking you wrapped your face

in the green scarf
the gray
and then the black
The waves carve your hearse and tomb
and toll your voyage out again again

NEWS FROM THE CABIN

1

Hairy was here.
He hung on a sumac seedpod.
Part of his double tail hugged the crimson
    scrotum under cockscomb leaves—
        or call it blushing lobster claw, that swatch—
        a toothy match to Hairy's red skullpatch.
Cried *peek!* Beaked it—chiseled the drupe.
His nostril I saw, slit in a slate whistle.
White-black dominoes clicked in his wings.
Bunched beneath the dangle he heckled with holes,
      bellysack soft, eye a brad, a red-flecked
      mallet his ball-peen head, his neck its haft.

2

Scurry was here.
He sat up like a six-inch bear,
      rocked on the porch with me;
      brought his own chair, his chow-haired tail.
Ate a cherry I threw.
Furry paunch, birchbark-snowy, pinecone-brown back,
      a jacket with sleeves to the digits.
Sat put, pert, neat, in his suit and his seat, for a minute,
      a frown between snub ears—bulb-eyed head
      toward me sideways, chewed.
Rocked, squeaked. Stored the stone in his cheek.
Finished, fell to all fours, a little roan couch;
      flurried paws loped him off, prone-bodied,
      tail turned torch, sail, scarf.

3

Then, Slicker was here.
Dipped down, cobalt and turquoise brushes
      fresh as paint. Gripped a pine-tassel,
      folded his flaunts, parted his pointed nib, and scrawled
      jeeah! on the air.
Japanned so smooth, his head-peak and all his shaft:
      harsh taunts from that dovey shape, soft tints—

nape and chin black-splintered, quilltips white-lashed.
Javelin-bird, he slurred his color,
     left his ink-bold word here; flashed off.
Morning prints his corvine noise elsewhere,
     while that green toss still quivers with his equipoise.

4

And Supple was here.
Lives nearby at the stump.
Trickled out from under, when the sun struck there.
Mud-and-silver-licked, his length—a single spastic muscle—
     slid over stones and twigs to a snuggle of roots, and hid.
I followed that elastic: loose
     unicolored knot, a noose he made as if unconscious.
Until my shadow touched him: half his curd
     shuddered, the rest lay chill.
I stirred: the ribbon raised a loop;
     its end stretched, then cringed like an udder;
     a bifid tongue, his only rapid, whirred
     in the vent; vertical pupils lit his hood.
That part, a groping finger, hinged, stayed upright.
Indicated what? That I stood
     in his light? I left the spot.

WAITING FOR *IT*

My cat jumps to the windowsill
and sits there still as a jug.
He's waiting for me, but I cannot be
coming, for I am in the room.

His snout, a gloomy V of patience,
pokes out into the sun.
The funnels of his ears expect
to be poured full of my footsteps.

It, the electric moment, a sweet
mouse, will appear; at his gray
eye's edge I'll be coming home
if he sits on the window-ledge.

It is here, I say, and call him
to my lap. Not a hair
in the gap of his ear moves.
His clay gaze stays steady.

That solemn snout says: *It*
is what is about to happen, not
what is already here.

ALMANAC

The hammer struck my nail, instead of nail.
A moon flinched into being. Omen-black,
it began its trail. Risen from horizon
on my thumb (no longer numb and indigo)
it waxed yellow, waned to a sliver that now
sets white, here at the rim I cut tonight.

I make it disappear, but mark its voyage
over my little oval ceiling that again
is cloudless, pink and clear. In the dark
quarter-inch of this moon before it arrived
at my nail's tip, an unmanned airship
dived 200 miles to the hem of space, and
vanished. At the place of Pharaoh Cheops'
tomb (my full moon floating yellow)
a boat for ferrying souls to the sun
was disclosed in a room sealed 5000 years.

Reaching whiteness, this moon-speck waned
while an April rained. Across the street,
a vine crept over brick up 14 feet. And
Einstein (who said there is no hitching
post in the universe) at 77 turned ghost.

THE CENTAUR

The summer that I was ten—
Can it be there was only one
summer that I was ten? It must

have been a long one then—
each day I'd go out to choose
a fresh horse from my stable

which was a willow grove
down by the old canal.
I'd go on my two bare feet.

But when, with my brother's jackknife,
I had cut me a long limber horse
with a good thick knob for a head,

and peeled him slick and clean
except a few leaves for the tail,
and cinched my brother's belt

around his head for a rein,
I'd straddle and canter him fast
up the grass bank to the path,

trot along in the lovely dust
that talcumed over his hoofs,
hiding my toes, and turning

his feet to swift half-moons.
The willow knob with the strap
jouncing between my thighs

was the pommel and yet the poll
of my nickering pony's head.
My head and my neck were mine,

yet they were shaped like a horse.
My hair flopped to the side
like the mane of a horse in the wind.

My forelock swung in my eyes,
my neck arched and I snorted.
I shied and skittered and reared,

stopped and raised my knees,
pawed at the ground and quivered.
My teeth bared as we wheeled

and swished through the dust again.
I was the horse and the rider,
and the leather I slapped to his rump

spanked my own behind.
Doubled, my two hoofs beat
a gallop along the bank,

the wind twanged in my mane,
my mouth squared to the bit.
And yet I sat on my steed

quiet, negligent riding,
my toes standing the stirrups,
my thighs hugging his ribs.

At a walk we drew up to the porch.
I tethered him to a paling.
Dismounting, I smoothed my skirt

and entered the dusky hall.
My feet on the clean linoleum
left ghostly toes in the hall.

Where have you been? said my mother.
Been riding, I said from the sink,
and filled me a glass of water.

What's that in your pocket? she said.
Just my knife. It weighted my pocket
and stretched my dress awry.

Go tie back your hair, said my mother,
and *Why is your mouth all green?*
Rob Roy, he pulled some clover
as we crossed the field, I told her.

THE POPLAR'S SHADOW

When I was little, when
the poplar was in leaf,
its shadow made a sheaf,
the quill of a great pen
dark upon the lawn
where I used to play.

Grown, and long away
into the city gone,
I see the pigeons print
a loop in air and, all
their wings reversing, fall
with silver undertint
like poplar leaves, their seams
in the wind blown.

Time's other side, shown
as a flipped coin, gleams
on city ground
when I see a pigeon's feather:
little and large together,
the poplar's shadow is found.

Staring at here,
and superposing then,
I wait for when.
What shapes will appear?
Will great birds swing
over me like gongs?
The poplar plume belongs
to what enormous wing?

FOUNTAIN PIECE

A bird
   is perched
      upon a wing

The wing
is stone
The bird
is real

A drapery
   falls about this form
      The form is stone
         The dress is rain

The pigeon preens his own
and does not know
he sits upon a wing
The angel does not feel
a relative among her large
feathers stretch
and take his span
in charge
and leave her there
with her cold
wings that cannot fold
while his fan
in air.

The fountain raining
   wets the stone
      but does not know it dresses
         an angel in its tresses

Her stone cheek smiles
and does not care
that real tears
flow there

THE ENGAGEMENT

When snow   cross
a wing   to where
is folded   I flow
over everything   in the rainbow

when night   seek me
a net   in the rock
dips us   break
in forget   that lock

when blue   meet me
my eye   in the wheel
leaks into   your thread
a sky   I'll feel

and floss   I'll come
your skin   to where you sink
is what the   in the tiger's
spiders spin   blink

when stone   and catch you
our veins   in the fish
are parted   with my strenuous
chains   wish

when prism   Find me
sun   in the flake
bends us   I will
one from one   wake

THE RED BIRD TAPESTRY

Now I put on the thimble of dream
    to stitch among leaves the red node of his body
and fasten here the few beads of his song.

Of the tree a cage of gilded spines
    to palace his scarlet, cathedral his cry,
and a ripple from his beak I sew,
    a banner bearing seven studs,
this scarf to be the morning that received his stain.

I do with thought instead of actuality
    for it has flown.
With glinting thimble I pull back, pull back
    that freak of scarlet to his throne:

To worship him, enchanted cherry to a tree
    that never bore such fruit—
who tore the veil of possibility
    and swung here for a day,
a never-colored bird, a never-music heard,
    who, doubly wanded then, looped away.

To find, in hollow of my throat, his call,
    and try his note on all the flutes of memory,
until that clear jet rinses me
    that was his single play—
for this I wear his daring and his royal eye.

Now perfected, arrested in absence—
    my needle laid by and spread my hand—
his claws on stems of my fingers fastened,
    rooted my feet and green my brow,
I drink from his beak the seven beads dropping:
    I am the cage that flatters him now.

THE SCHOOL OF DESIRE

Unloosed, unharnessed, turned back to the wild by love,
the ring you cantered round with forelock curled,
the geometric music of this world
dissolved and, in its place,
alien as snow to tropic tigers, amphitheatric space,
you will know the desert's freedom, wind and sun
rough-currying your mane, the plenitude
of strong caresses on your body nude.

Released to run from me. Then will I stand
alone in the hoof-torn ring,
lax in my hand
as wine leaked out the thin whip of my will,
and gone the lightning-string
between your eye and mine.

Our discipline was mutual and the art
that spun our dual beauty. While you wheeled
in flawless stride apart,
I, in glittering boots to the fulcrum heeled,
hardly signaled: your prideful head
plunged to the goad of love-looks sharper than ice.

I gloated on the palomino of your flanks, the nice
sprightliness of pace,
your posture like Apollo's steed. I stood my place
as in a chariot,
held the thong of studded light, the lariat
that made you halt, or longer leap, or faster.
But you have bridled me, bright master.

On wild, untrampled slopes you will be monarch soon,
and I the mount that carries you to those high
prairies steeped in noon.
In the arena where your passion will be spent

in loops of speed, sky's indigo unbounded
by the trainer's tent,
instead of oboes, thunder's riddle,
rain for the racing fifes, I will be absent.

When orchestras of air shall vault you
to such freedom, joy and power,
I will cut the whip that sent you there, will put
away the broken ring, and shut
the school of my desire.

TWO-PART PEAR ABLE

1. Something Missing

In a country where
every tree is a pear tree
it is a shock to see
one tree
(a pear tree undoubtedly
for its leaves are the leaves
of a pear)
that shows no pears

It is a fairly tall tree
sturdy
capable looking
its limbs strong its leaves glossy
its posture in fact exceptionally
pleasing

but there
among the true pear trees
all of which show pears

the pear tree with no pears
appears (to say the least)
unlikely
and therefore
unlovely

You see
those globes invariably
grow in the trees of that country
There are no other kinds of trees
and pears in the pear trees
are what make them trees
as much
(no even more than)
their leaves
Otherwise they would be named
leaf trees

Pears are what the trees *have*
The leaves are accessory
They are there
to set off the shapes
and colors of the fruits
and shade them
(naturally)
and shelter them
It is as if the trees
were great cool nests for the pears
So that a nest
like the rest (apparently)
but empty
is inconceivable
Like seeing a ghost
or at most a body
without bones

It is a shock
and a pity to see
a pear tree
that can't be
but is

2. Something Added Is Worse

But in another country
where there
are trees just trees
and no one has ever seen
a fruit tree
of any kind
(much less specifically
a pear tree)
suppose a *pear* tree

(This country must be
entirely imaginary
you say and we agree
The other's unlikely
but could be)

Suppose suddenly
in between leaves
(that are the "fruits" actually)
another sort of a leaf
but differently
shaped and colored
heavier
and depending from a gross
stem were discovered
And then more and more

And finally
it is seen that this tree
is infested with pears
(not yet named of course)
hidden
but obviously
getting bigger
growing there with the leaves

And someone says
How horrible

these leaves are turning into
into *fruits*
(fortuitously
inventing an aggressive
name for it)

There will be
general revulsion won't there?
There will be
demand for expulsion

which could easily
succeed
for the time being

And in that country's
dictionary
it will be
a long while before you see
the word *pear*

A LAKE SCENE

So innocent this scene, I feel I see it
   with a deer's eye,
uncovering a first secret from this shore.
   I think of the smoothest thing:
the inside of a young thigh,
   or the line of a torso when, supine,
the pectoral sheathe crosses the armpit
   to the outflung arm;
at the juncture of lake and hills, that zone,
   the lowest hill in weavings
of fainter others overlaid,
   is a pelvis in shadow.

The hazel waves slip toward me,
   the far arcade
honed by the sunset; nothing tears
   the transparent skin that water
and sky and, between them,
   the undulant horizon wears.
No contest here, no roughness,
   no threat,
the wind's lick mild as the lake's,
   the rock I lean on, moss-round
as that silhouette
   in the thwart of the opposite shore;
spruce and fir snug-wool its folds.

My eye goes there, to the source
of a first secret. I would be inheritor
   of the lamb's way and the deer's,
my thrust take from the ground
   I tread or lie on. In thighs of trees,
in recumbent stones, in the loins
   of beasts is found
that line my own nakedness carried.
   Here, in an Eden of the mind,
I would remain among my kind,
   to lake and hill, to tree and beast married.

FOREST

The pines, aggressive as erect tails of cats,
bob their tips when the wind freshens.

An alert breath like purring stirs below,
where I move timid over humps of hair,

crisp, shadow-brindled, heaving as if
exhilarated muscular backs felt

the wisps of my walking. Looking to sky,
glaring then closing between the slow

lashes of boughs, I feel observed:
up high are oblong eyes that know,

as their slits of green light
expand, squeeze shut, expand,

that I stand here. Suddenly I go,
flick-eyed, hurrying over fur

needles that whisper as if they weren't dead.
My neck-hairs rise. The feline forest grins

behind me. Is it about to follow?
Which way out through all these whiskered yawns?

HER MANAGEMENT

She does not place, relate, or name
the objects of her hall,
nor bother to repair her ceiling,
sweep her floor, or paint a wall
symmetrical with mountains;

cylindrical her tent
is pitched of ocean on one side
and—rakish accident—
forest on the other.
Granular, her rug

of many marbles, or of roots,
or needles, or a bog—
outrageous in its pattern;
the furniture is pine
and oak and birch and beech and elm;

the water couch is fine.
Mottled clouds, and lightning rifts,
leaking stars, and whole
gushing moons despoil her roof.
Contemptuous of control,

she lets a furnace burn all day,
she lets the winds be wild.
Broken, rotting, shambled things
lie where they like, are piled
on the same tables with her sweets,

her fruits, and scented stuffs.
Her management is beauty.
Of careless silks and roughs,
rumpled rocks, the straightest rain,
blizzards, roses, crows,

April lambs and graveyards
she *chances* to compose
a rich and sloven manor.
Her prosperous tapestries
are too effusive in design

for our analyses—
we, who through her textures move,
we specks upon her glass,
who try to place, relate and name
all things within her mass.

ORDER OF DIET

1

Salt of the soil and liquor of the rock
is all the thick land's food and mead.
And jaws of cattle grip up
stuffs of pasture for their bellies' need.
We, at table with our knives,
cut apart and swallow other lives.

2

The stone is milked to feed the tree;
the log is killed when the flame is hungry.
To arise in the other's body?
Flank of the heifer we glut, we spend
to redden our blood. Then do we send
her vague spirit higher? Does the grain
come to better fortune in our brain?

3

Ashes find their way to green;
the worm is raised into the wing;
the sluggish fish to muscle slides;
eventual chemistry will bring
the lightning bug to the shrewd toad's eye.
It is true no thing of earth can die.

4

What then feeds on us? On our blood
and delectable flesh: the flood
of flower to fossil, coal to snow,
genes of glacier and volcano,
and our diamond souls that are bent
upward? To what Beast's intent
are we His fodder and nourishment?

THE CLOUD-MOBILE

Above my face is a map.
Continents form and fade.
Blue countries, made
on a white sea, are erased,
and white countries traced
on a blue sea.

It is a map that moves:
faster than real,
but so slow.
Only my watching proves
that island has being,
or that bay.

It is a model of time.
Mountains are wearing away,
coasts cracking,
the ocean spills over,
then new hills
heap into view
with river-cuts of blue
between them.

It is a map of change.
This is the way things are
with a stone or a star.
This is the way things go,
hard or soft,
swift or slow.

DEATH, GREAT SMOOTHENER

Death,
great smoothener,
maker of order,
arrester, unraveler, sifter and changer;
death, great hoarder;
student, stranger, drifter, traveler,
flyer and nester all caught at your border;
death,
great halter;
blackener and frightener,
reducer, dissolver,
seizer and welder of younger with elder,
waker with sleeper,
death, great keeper
of all that must alter;
death,
great heightener,
leaper, evolver,
great smoothener,
great whitener!

DECIDING

Deciding to go on digging doing it
what they said outside wasn't any use
Inside hiding it made it get ambitious
Like a potato in a dark bin
it grew white grabbers for light
out of its navel eyes not priding
itself much just deciding
it wasn't true inside what they said
outside those bumps were

All humped alike dumped inside
slumped in burlap said
roots are no good out of ground
a fruit's crazy to want to be a flower
Besides it's sin changing the given shape
Bursting the old brown skin is suicide
Wishing to taste like a tulip
sip colored light
outside thumps said isn't right

Deciding to keep on striding
from inside bursting the bin-side
poking out wishes for delicious opposites
turning blind eyes to strong fingers
touching meaning more than sight
the navel scars of weaning
used for something finally
Deciding to go on digging doing it

WORKING ON WALL STREET

What's left of the sunset's watered blood
settles between the slabs of Wall Street.
Winter rubs the sky bruise-blue as flesh.
We head down into the subway, glad
the cars are padded with bodies so we
keep warm. Emptied from tall closets
where we work, on the days' shelves
reached by elevators, the heap of us,
pressed by iron sides, dives forward under
the city—parcels shipped out in a trunk.

The train climbs from its cut to the trestle.
Sunset's gone. Those slabs across the murky
river have shrunk to figurines, reflecting
the blush of neon—a dainty tableau, all
pink, on the dresser-top of Manhattan—
eclipsed as we sink into the tunnel.
The train drops and flattens for the long
bore under Brooklyn.

Night, a hiatus hardly real, tomorrow
this double rut of steel will racket us back
to the city. We, packages in the trade
made day after day, will tumble out of
hatches on the Street, to be met by swags
of wind that scupper off those roofs
(their upper windows blood-filled by the sun).
Delivered into lobbies, clapped into upgoing
cages, sorted to our compartments, we'll be
stamped once more for our wages.

LOOKING UPTOWN

All cars run one way: toward the point of the wedge
where the sky is pinched
in the meeting of perpendiculars.
Over mats of shadow, through rents of sun,
the cars run, with a sound of ripping silk
in the gape of the avenue,
to cram where it narrows far uptown.
The metallic back of something scaly
oozes there in its trap.

Here in the foreground: gigantic terraces
of stone to left and right, inlaid with squares
of mirror; and the suede shadows mimic on cement
angular rhomboids, flat parapets,
so that the cars purr over wide checkers.

Along the corridor, the eye, as well, must race,
drawn by a stream of horizontal threads
fastened to that far blue slice.
At every crossing, pairs of hooded lights
decide to let the cars proceed.
But, in the vise, a glinting lizard pack
strangles, drained of speed,
while the free eye dives on, true and straight,
up the open vertical, to swallow space.

TO THE STATUE

The square-heeled boat sets off for the Statue.
People are stuck up tight as asparagus stalks
inside the red rails (ribbons tying the bunch).

The tips, their rigid heads against the fog,
all yearn toward the Statue; dents of waves
all minimize and multiply to where

she, fifteen minutes afar (a cooky-tin-shaped
mother-doll) stands without a feature
except her little club of flame.

Other boats pass the promenade. It's exciting
to watch the water heave up, clop the pier,
and even off: a large unsteady belly,

oil-scaled, gasping, then breathing normally.
On the curved horizon, faded shapes of ships,
with thready regalia, cobweb a thick sky.

Nearer, a spluttering bubble over the water
(a mosquito's skeletal hindpart, wings detached
and fused to whip on top like a child's whirltoy)

holds two policemen. They're seated in the air,
serge, brass-buttoned paunches behind glass,
serene, on rubber runners, sledding fog.

Coming back, framed by swollen pilings,
the boat is only inches wide, and flat.
Stalk by stalk, they've climbed into her head

(its bronze is green out there, and hugely spiked)
and down her winding spine into their package,
that now bobs forward on the water's mat.

Soon three-dimensional, colored like a drum,
red-staved, flying a dotted flag,
its rusty iron toe divides the harbor;

sparkling shavings curl out from the bow.
Their heads have faces now. They've been to the Statue.
She has no face from here, but just a fist.
(I think of the flame carved like an asparagus tip.)

AT EAST RIVER

Tugboat: A large shoe
shuffles the floor of water,
leaving a bright scrape.

Floating Gulls: Ballet slippers, dirty-white,
walk awkward backward.
Bobbing closer: yellow-pointed painted
wooden shoes.

The Bay: Flat, shiny, rustling
like parquet under the bridge's
balustrade of gray garlands.

On the Bridge: Slow skates of cars (a distant whisper)
and the long swishing foot of a train.

A Plane: Turns on its elegant heel:
a spark, a click
of steel on blue.

That Steamer: The top of a short boot, red and black,
budging deep water wading to the sea.

Brooklyn: A shelf of old shoes
needing repair,
but clean knots of smoke
are being tied and untied.

WATER PICTURE

In the pond in the park
all things are doubled:
Long buildings hang and
wriggle gently. Chimneys
are bent legs bouncing
on clouds below. A flag
wags like a fishhook
down there in the sky.

The arched stone bridge
is an eye, with underlid
in the water. In its lens
dip crinkled heads with hats
that don't fall off. Dogs go by,
barking on their backs.
A baby, taken to feed the
ducks, dangles upside-down,
a pink balloon for a buoy.

Treetops deploy a haze of
cherry bloom for roots,
where birds coast belly-up
in the glass bowl of a hill;
from its bottom a bunch
of peanut-munching children
is suspended by their
sneakers, waveringly.

A swan, with twin necks
forming the figure 3,
steers between two dimpled
towers doubled. Fondly
hissing, she kisses herself,
and all the scene is troubled:
water-windows splinter,
tree-limbs tangle, the bridge
folds like a fan.

ZAMBESI AND RANEE

Because their mothers refused to nurse them, the two female
animals in this compartment were reared together by hand
from early infancy . . . They are firm friends and strongly resent
separation. While Zambesi, the lion, is inclined to be rough and
aggressive, Ranee, the tiger, easily dominates her.
—*From a plaque at the Bronx Zoo*

The tiger looks the younger and more male,
her body ribbed with staves as black as Bengal's
   in the next den. Clear green her eyes,
   in the great three-cornered head, set slantwise;
her hips as lean, her back as straight,
she's a velvet table when she walks, and able
   to bound ten feet to the level where her meat
   is flung at feeding time.

The lion, square-bodied, heavy-pelted, less grand,
her maneless, round-eared head held low,
   slouches and rocks in sand-colored nakedness,
   drag-bellied, watchful and slow; her yellow eyes
jealous, something morose in the down-hook
   of her jaw; her tail, balled at the end
   like a riding crop, taps at the bars.

They twine their shared pavilion, each spine
tracing an opposite figure eight. Paired females,
   they avoid each other's touch; but if, passing,
   as much as a whisker of that black-and-orange head
grazes the lion's flank, her topaz eye narrows:
   irascibly she turns with slugger's paw
   to rake the ear of her mate.

Then rampant they wrestle; rich snarls
in coils pour from their throats and nostrils.
   Like soft boulders the bodies tumble each other down.
   Then, not bothering to rise, they lounge,
chest to chest. It is not hate embroils them,
but that neither will be humble to the other.
   Nor will the tiger, in earnest, test her quickness
   against the lion's weight.

Few sights can still surprise us in the zoo,
    though this is the place for marvels.
These odd heroines do attract us. Why?
Crouched on sinewy elbows, sphinxes, they project
    vast boredom. Those still heads outstare
    some horizon of catlike time, while we, in vain,
expect a gleam from eye to eye between them,
a posture of affection, or some clue . . .

Bemused at the bars, some watchers smile and read
Zambesi and Ranee upon their card;
they might ring the bell, introduce themselves
    and be welcome. The life these ladies lead,
upon their stage, repeats itself behind the walls
    of many city streets; silent, or aloud,
    the knowing crowd snickers.

Refused to nurse them, simpering mothers read,
and tighten the hold on Darling's hand: "Look
    at the pussycats!" they coax, they croon,
    but blushing outrage heats their cheeks—
that this ménage calls down no curse,
not only is excused, but celebrated:
    They'd prefer these captives punished, who
    seem to wear the brand some captivated humans do.

EARLY MORNING: CAPE COD

We wake to double blue:
an ocean without sail,
sky without a clue
of white.
Morning is a veil
sewn of only two
threads, one pale,
one bright.

We bathe as if in ink,
but peacock-eyed and clear;
a roof of periwink
goes steep
into a bell of air
vacant to the brink.
Far as we can peer
is deep

royal blue and shy
iris, queen and king
colors of low
and high.
Then dips
a sickle wing,
we hear a hinged cry:
taut as from a sling

downwhips
a taunting gull.
And now across our gaze
a snowy hull
appears;
triangles
along its stays
break out to windpulls.

With creaking shears
the bright
gulls cut the veil
in two,
and many a clue
on scalloped sail
dots with white
our double blue.

THE EVEN SEA

Meekly the sea
now plods to shore:
white-faced cattle used to their yard,
the waves, with weary knees,
come back from bouldered hills
of high water,

where all the gray, rough day they seethed like bulls,
till the wind laid down its goads
at shift of tide, and sundown
gentled them; with lowered necks
they amble up the beach
as to their stalls.

THE PROMONTORY MOMENT

Think of only now, and how this pencil,
tilted in the sand, might be a mast,
its shadow to an ant marking the sun's place;
little and vast are the same to that big eye
that sees no shadow.

Think how future and past, afloat on an ocean
of breath, linked as one island,
might coexist with the promontory moment
around the sun's disk — for that wide eye
knows no distance or divide.

Over your shoulder in the circular cove, the sea,
woven by swimmers' gaudy heads, pulses an indigo
wing that pales at its frothy edge;
and, far out, sails as slow as clouds
change bodies as they come about.

Look at the standing gull, his pincered beak
yellow as this pencil, a scarlet streak beneath the tip,
the puff of his chest bowl-round and white,
his cuff-button eye of ice and jet
fixed on the slicing waves; shingle-snug, his gray wing
tucked to his side; aloft, that plumpness,
whittled flat, sits like a kite.

Turn to where fishermen rise from a neck
of rock, rooted and still, rods played like spouts
from their hips, until, beneath the chips of waves,
a cheek rips on the barb, a silver soul is flipped
from the sea's cool home into fatal air.

Close your eyes and hear the toss of the waves'
innumerable curls on the brow of the world—
that head is shaggy as Samson's, and three-fourths
furred. And *now* is eternal in beard and tress
piled green, blown white on churned sand,
the brand of the past an ephemeral smutch
of brown seaweed cast back to the sucking surf.

Tomorrow the marge is replaced
by a lace of shells, to be gathered again
by the hairy sea when it swells; here nothing is built
or grown, and nothing destroyed; and the buoyed
mind dares to enmirror itself,
as the prone body, bared to the sun,
is undone of its cares.

The eye, also a sun, wanders,
and all that it sees it owns;
the filled sail, tacking the line between water
and sky, its mast as high as this pencil,
becomes the gull's dropped quill, and the fleece
of the wave, and the sea robin's arc
now stilled on the rock.

THE TIDE AT LONG POINT

The sea comes up and the sun goes over
    The sea goes out and the sun falls
The stubby shadow of the lighthouse pales
    stretches to a finger and inches east
The wind lifts from off the sea
    and curries and curries the manes of the dunes
The pipers and the terns skate over
    tweaking the air with their talk
In sky clean as a cat-licked dish
    clouds are sandbars bared by ebbing blue

The hourglass is reversed

The sea comes up and the moon peers over
    The sea goes out and the moon swells
The shadow of the lighthouse thick as a boot
    is swiped by a whiskered beam
The wind licks at the jetty stones
    The pipers and terns hunch on the spit
hiding their necks and stilted feet
    The sky has caught a netful of stars
The moon is a dory trolling them in

The hourglass is reversed

The sea comes up and the moon tips under
    The sea goes out and the sun looms
The sun is a schooner making for harbor
    Shallops of cloud are adrift in the west
The wind gallops the waves to a lather
    and lashes the grass that shines on the dunes
The lighthouse looks at its twin in the water
    The pipers and terns preen on its brow

EXECUTIONS

I walk out on thongs of shadow,
my back to the morning sun,
the pines' dark quivers running up along their bow
of sky: taut blue about to twang
with the anguish of summer, shot.
October's target-mark on every leaf,
on points of dew my shadow rips;
light pierces wings of jays in flight:
they shout my grief.

Ring, locusts: murder is prepared;
shorn fair pine hair litters the ground;
swords already have beheaded mushrooms:
black necks rot in these sunny grottos
that sumac, blood-beaded, drapes.
And ghostly fern here frightens me,
spanned like my light-catching hands,
a design for urns.

By stride escaped to the meadow,
I think that mound, that haul of sun,
a health of yellow, still safe from killer shadow,
but all is beaten flat: torn shucks
in the flogging place, pale corpses
surpliced with light.
Then, hearse-horns of macabre crows sweep over;
gibbet-masks they cut on blue.
I wade in husks, in broken shafts of arrows.

SPRING UNCOVERED

Gone the scab of ice that kept it snug,
the lake is naked.

Skins of cloud on torn blue:
sky is thin.

A cruelty, the ribs of trees
ribboned by sun's organdy.

Forsythia's yellow, delicate rags,
flip in the wind.

Wind buckles the face of the lake;
it flinches under a smack of shot.

Robbed of stoic frost, grass
bleeds from gaffs of the wind.

Rock, ridging the lake,
unchapped of its snowcloth, quakes.

But autumn fruits upon the water,
plumage of plum, and grape, and pumpkin bills:

Two mallards ride, are sunny baskets;
they bear ripe light.

And a grackle, fat as burgundy,
gurgles on a limb.

His bottle-glossy feathers
shrug off the wind.

from Another Animal

EVOLUTION

the stone
would like to be
Alive like me

the rooted tree
longs to be Free

the mute beast
envies my fate
Articulate

on this ball
half dark
half light
i walk Upright
i lie prone
within the night

beautiful each Shape
to see
wonderful each Thing
to name
here a stone
there a tree
here a river
there a Flame

marvelous to Stroke
the patient beasts
within their yoke

how i Yearn
for the lion
in his den
though he spurn
the touch of men

the longing
that i know
is in the Stone also
it must be

the same that rises
in the Tree
the longing
in the Lion's call
speaks for all

oh to Endure
like the stone
sufficient
to itself alone

or Reincarnate
like the tree
be born each spring
to greenery

or like the lion
without law
to roam the Wild
on velvet paw

but if walking
i meet
a Creature like me
on the street
two-legged
with human face
to recognize
is to Embrace

wonders pale
beauties dim
during my delight
with Him

an Evolution strange
two Tongues touch
exchange
a Feast unknown
to stone
or tree or beast

FEEL LIKE A BIRD

feel like A Bird
understand
he has no hand

instead A Wing
close-lapped
mysterious thing

in sleeveless coat
he halves The Air
skipping there
like water-licked boat

lands on star-toes
finger-beak in
feather-pocket
finds no Coin

in neat head like
seeds in A Quartered
Apple eyes join
sniping at opposites
stereoscope The Scene
Before

close to floor giddy
no arms to fling
A Third Sail
spreads for calm
his tail

hand better
than A Wing?
to gather A Heap
to count
to clasp A Mate?

or leap
lone-free and mount
on muffled shoulders
to span A Fate?

LION

In the bend of your mouth soft murder
    in the flints of your eyes
    the sun-stained openings of caves
Your nostrils breathe the ordained air
    of chosen loneliness

Magnificently maned as the lustrous savannah
    your head heavy with heraldic curls
    wears a regal frown between the brows

The wide bundle of your chest
    your loose-skinned belly frilled with fur
    you carry easily sinuously pacing on suede paws

Between tight thighs
    under the thick root of your tufted tail
    situated like a full-stoned fruit beneath a bough
    the quiver of your never-used malehood is slung

You pace in dung on cement
    the bars flick past your eyeballs
    fixed beyond the awestruck stares of children
Watching you they remember their fathers
    the frightening hairs in their fathers' ears

Young girls remember lovers too timid and white
    and I remember how I played lion with my brothers
    under the round yellow-grained table
    the shadow our cave in the lamplight

Your beauty burns the brain
    though your paws slue on foul cement
    the fetor of captivity you do right to ignore
    the bars too an illusion

Your heroic paranoia plants you in the African jungle
    pacing by the cool water-hole as dawn streaks the sky
    and the foretaste of the all-day hunt
    is sweet as yearling's blood
    in the corners of your lips

SUN

With your masculine stride
   you tread insidious clouds and glide
   to the unobstructed parapet of noon-blue

   ruthless rip through cumulous veils of sloth
   spurn their sly caresses and erect
   an immediate stairway to passion's splendid throne

From yourself you fling your own earth-seed
   and orbits organize in the wombless infinite
   for your discipled planets

   radiant boys
   that imitate your stamping feet
   in the elliptic dance of fire

You are not moon-dependent on desire
   in rotund rhythm leashed to a mineral despot
   like that satellite in female furrow sown

   that white rib plucked from Adam-earth
   but appended still
   eclipsed beneath his dark chest
   writhing to his will

   one-sided shield turned to the urgent tide
   compelled to yield to the night-sky slime
   she that marble-smiling sinks in moss
At dawn rubbed thin a mutilate
   she melts and faints in the cold cloud curd

   while you are up afork the first ringing word
   of potent joy the sharp-tined golden shout
   divine and glistering your beard with dewy flames
   sprinting to the pantheon and your godlike games

HORSES IN CENTRAL PARK

Colors of horses like leaves or stones
or wealthy textures
liquors of light

The skin of a plum that's more than ripe
sheathes a robust
cloven rump

Frosty plush of lilies
for another's head
ears and nostrils funneled are their cones

Of sere October leaves
this gaunt roan's hide
freckled dun and red

Here's a mole-gray back
and darker dappled haunch
tail and forelock mauve like smoke

This coal-colored stallion
flake of white on his brow
is slippery silk in the sun

Fox-red bay
and buckskin blond as wheat
Burgundy mare with tasseled mane of jet

Sober chestnut burnished
by his sweat
to veined and glowing oak

Seal-brown mustang
with stocking-feet
Pinto in patched and hooded domino

Naked palomino
is smooth peeled willow
or marble under water or clean morning snow

MORNINGS INNOCENT

I wear your smile upon my lips
arising on mornings innocent
Your laughter overflows my throat
Your skin is a fleece about me
With your princely walk I salute the sun
People say I am handsome

Arising on mornings innocent
birds make the sound of kisses
Leaves flicker light and dark like eyes

I melt beneath the magnet of your gaze
Your husky breath insinuates my ear
Alert and fresh as grass I wake

and rise on mornings innocent
The strands of the wrestler
run golden through my limbs
I cleave the air with insolent ease
With your princely walk I salute the sun
People say I am handsome

HE THAT NONE CAN CAPTURE

The acrobat astride his swing in space
the pole rolled under his instep
catches the pits of his knees
is lipped by his triangled groin
fits the fold of his hard-carved buttocks

Long-thighed tight-hipped he drops
head-down and writhes erect
glazed smooth by speed a twirled top
sits immobile in the void

Gravity outwhipped squeezed like dough
is kneaded to his own design
a balance-egg at the plexus of his bowels
counteracting vertigo

Empty of fear and therefore without weight
he walks a wedge of steeper air
indifferent to the enormous stare
of onlookers in rims of awe below

Drumbeats are solid blocks beneath him
Strong brass horn-tones prolong him
on glittering stilts

Self-hurled he swims the color-stippled height
where nothing but whisks of light
can reach him

At night he is my lover

TO CONFIRM A THING

To confirm a Thing and give thanks
                    to the stars that named me
and fixed me in the Wheel of heaven
            my fate pricked out in the Boxer's chest
in the hips curled over the Horse
                Though girled in an apple-pink month
and the moon hornless
                the Brothers glitter in my wristbones
At ankle and knee I am set astride
                        and made stubborn in love

In the equal Night where oracular beasts
                            the planets depose
and our Selves assume their orbits
            I am flung where the Girdle's double studs
grant my destiny
                    I am the Athletes in that zone
My thighs made marble-hard
                    uncouple only to the Archer
with his diametrical bow
                    who prances in the South
himself a part of his horse
            His gemmed arrow splits the hugging Twins

The moon was gelded on that other night as well
            Oh his feeble kingdom we will tip over
If our feet traverse the Milky Way
        the earth's eccentric bead on which we balance
is small enough to hide between our toes
                its moon a mote that the Long Eye
is hardly conscious of
                        nor need we be

278

The tough the sensuous Body our belief
                         and fitting the pranks of Zeus
to this our universe
               we are Swans or Bulls as the music turns us
We are Children incorrigible and perverse
                     who hold our obstinate seats
on heaven's carousel
                   refusing our earth's assignment
refusing to descend
                to beget such trifles of ourselves
as the gibbous Mothers do
                We play in the Den of the Gods
and snort at death

Then let me by these signs
                    maintain my magnitude
as the candid Centaur his dynasty upholds
                  And in the Ecliptic Year
our sweet rebellions
                shall not be occulted but remain
coronals in heaven's Wheel

THE GARDEN AT ST. JOHN'S

Behind the wall of St. John's in the city
in the shade of the garden the Rector's wife
walks with her baby a girl and the first
its mouth at her neck seeking and sucking
in one hand holding its buttocks its skull
cupped by the other her arms like a basket
of tenderest fruit and thinks as she fondles
the nape of the infant its sweat is like dew
like dew and its hair is as soft as soft
as down as the down in the wingpits of angels

The little white dog with the harlequin eye
his tail like a thumb feet nimble as casters
scoots in the paths of the garden's meander
behind the wall of St. John's in the city
a toy deposed from his place in her arms
by this doll of the porcelain bone
this pale living fruit without stone

She walks where the wrinkling tinkling fountain
laps at the granite head of a monk
where dip the slippery noses of goldfish
and tadpoles flip from his cuspid mouth
A miracle surely the young wife thinks
from such a hard husband a tender child
and thinks of his black sleeves on the hymnbook
inside the wall of St. John's in the city
the Ah of his stiff mouth intoning Amen
while the organ prolongs its harmonious snore

Two trees like swans' necks twine in the garden
beside the wall of St. John's in the city
Brooding and cool in the shade of the garden
the scrolled beds of ivy glitter like vipers

A miracle surely this child and this garden
  of succulent green in the broil of the city
she thinks as setting the bird-cries apart
  she hears from beneath the dark spirals of ivy
under the wall of St. John's in the city
  the rectal rush and belch of the subway
roiling the corrugate bowels of the city
  and sees in the sky the surgical gleam
of an airplane stitching its way to the West
  above the wall of St. John's in the city
ripping its way through the denim air

HORSE AND SWAN FEEDING

Half a swan a horse is
 how he slants his muzzle to the clover
 forehead dips in a leaf-lake
 as she the sweet worm sips
 spading the velvet mud-moss with her beak
His chin like another hoof he plants
 to preen the feathered green
Up now is tossed her brow from the water-mask
With airy muscles black and sleek
 his neck is raised curried with dew
He shudders to the tail delicately
 sways his mane wind-hurried
Shall he sail or stay?
Her kingly neck on her male
 imperturbable white steed-like body
 rides stately away

BOY IN CANOE

In pod-shaped canoe
on the spanking lake
he propels his cradle
through uterine blue
his arms tatooed with
Grace & Force
the scoop of his long chest
Light & Strong
as the shell

Yellow his head
as if pollen-dusted
Stern-innocent his eyes
are turned to the fierce
sun's shield
unmindful of Medusas he must
pierce or yield to
voyage done

Between his thighs
like a young frog
in a loose fist
precious lies his genital
and pulsing in their
pouches wait
the little gold grains
of giant's teeth
to burrow into Dark & Wet
at summer's end
at the lake's bend

ANY OBJECT

any Object before the Eye
can fill the space can occupy
the supple frame of eternity

my Hand before me such
tangents reaches into Much
root and twig extremes can touch

any Hour can be the all
expanding like a cunning Ball
to a Vast from very small

skull and loin the twin-shaped Cup
store the glittering grainery up
for all the sandy stars to sup

any Single becomes the More
multiples sprout from alpha's core
from Vase of legend vessels of lore

to this pupil dark and wild
where lives the portrait of a Child
let me then be reconciled

germ of the first Intent to be
i am and must be seen to see
then every New descends from me

uncoiling into Motion i
start a massive panoply
the anamolecular atoms fly

and spread through ether like a foam
appropriating all the Dome
of absoluteness for my home

ORGANS

hidden in the hair
the spiral Ear
waits to Suck sound

and sly beneath its
ledge the Eye to Spear
the fish of light

the Mouth's a hole
and yet a Cry for
love for loot

with every stolen
breath the Snoot
Supposes roses

nose tongue fishing
eye's Crouched
in the same hutch

nibbling lips and
funnel's there
in the legs' lair
carnivora of Touch

SATANIC FORM

Numerals forkmarks of Satan
Triangles circles squares
hieroglyphs of death
Things invented
abortions smelling of the forge
licked to gruesome smoothness by the lathe
Things metallic or glass
frozen twisted flattened
stretched to agonized bubbles
Bricks beams receptacles vehicles
forced through fire hatched to unwilling form
Oh blasphemies
Time caught in a metal box
Incongruous the rigid clucking tongue
the needled hands the 12-eyed face
against the open window past which drops the night
like a dark lake on end or flowing hair
Night unanimous over all the city
The knuckled fist of the heart opening and closing
Flower and stone not cursed with symmetry
Cloud and shadow not doomed to shape and fixity
The intricate body of man without rivet or nail
or the terrible skirl of the screw
Oh these are blessed
Satanic form geometry of death
The lariat around the neck of space
The particles of chaos in the clock
The bottle of the yellow liquor light
that circumvents the sifting down of night
Oh love the juice in the green stem growing
we cannot synthesize
It corrodes in phials and beakers
evaporates in the hot breath of industry
escapes to the air and the dew
returns to the root of the unborn flower
Oh Satan cheated of your power

MORTAL SURGE

We are eager
We pant
We whine like whips cutting the air
The frothing sea
the roaring furnace
the jeweled eyes of animals call to us
and we stand frozen
moving neither forward nor back

In the breathless wedge between night and dawn
when the rill of blood pauses at the sluice of the heart
either to advance or retreat
the stars stare at us face to face
penetrating even the disguise of our nakedness
daring us to make the upward leap
effortless as falling
if only we relax the bowstring of our will

We seek the slippery flesh of other men
expecting to be comforted
or to be punished
or to be delighted beyond imagined delights
to be made clean
or to be baptized in the cool font of evil

We believe in the meeting of lips
in the converging of glances
that a talisman is given
that we shall arise anew
be healed and made whole
or be torn at last from our terrible womb-twin
our very self

We are loved in the image of the dead
We love in the image of the never-born
We shudder to beget with child
We shudder not to beget with child

We scream in the doorway of our beginning
We weep at the exit gate

We are alone and never alone
bound and never secured
let go and never freed
We would dance and are hurled
would build and are consumed
We are dragged backward by the past
jerked forward by the future

Our earth a bloody clot of the sun's cataclysm
sun a severed limb of a shattered universe
In fission
explosion
In separation
congealment

STONY BEACH

The sea like Demosthenes' mouth
champs upon these stones
whose many stumblings make him suave
The argument molded monotonously by all his lips
in a parliament of overlappings
is vocal but incomprehensible because never finished

Listen listen there is nothing to learn from the sea
Listen he is lucid in sound only
convinces with broken phrases that wizardly
the waves round out in a rune over riddling stones

Beginning again and again with a great *A*
a garbled alphabet he lisps and groans
The insistent eloquence of echoes
has no omega

THE KEY TO EVERYTHING

Is there anything I can do
or has everything been done
or do
you prefer somebody else to do
it or don't
you trust me to do
it right or is it hopeless and no one can do
a thing or do
you suppose I don't
really want to do
it and am just saying that or don't
you hear me at all or what?

You're
waiting for
the right person the doctor or
the nurse the father or
the mother or
the person with the name you keep
mumbling in your sleep
that no one ever heard of there's no one
named that really
except yourself maybe

If I knew what your
name was I'd
prove it's your
own name spelled backwards or
twisted in some way the one you
keep mumbling but you
won't tell me your
name or
don't you know it
yourself that's it
of course you've
forgotten or
never quite knew it or
weren't willing to believe it

Then there *is* something I
can do I
can find your name for you
that's the key to everything once you'd
repeat it clearly you'd
come awake you'd
get up and walk knowing where you're
going where you
came from

And you'd
love me
after that or would you
hate me?
no once you'd
get there you'd
remember and love me
of course I'd
be gone by then I'd
be far away

A WISH

Out of an hour I built a hut
  and like a Hindu sat
    immune in the wind of time

From a hair I made a path
  and walked and both
    rock and wilderness became

my space and thoroughfare
  With sorrow for a skin
    I felt no wound

Pleasant power like a nut
    ripened and split within me
      Where there had been wrath

it loosened all the world
  to quiet noonday
    My face in the rock my name

on the wildest tree
  My flesh the heath
    of a peaceful clime

A DREAM

I was a god and self-enchanted
I stood in a cabinet in the living wood
The doors were carved with the sign of the lizard
whose eye unblinks on emptiness
whose head turns slower than a tooth grows

I wore a mask of skin-thin silver
My hair was frenzied foam stiffened to ice
My feet gloved in petals of imperishable flowers
were hoofs and colder than hammers

I lived by magic
A little bag in my chest held a whirling stone
so hot it was past burning
so radiant it was blinding

When the moon rose worn and broken
her face like a coin endlessly exchanged
in the hands of the sea
her ray fell upon the doors which opened
and I walked in the living wood
The leaves turned bronze and the moss to marble

At morning I came back to my cabinet
It was a tree in the daylight
the lizard a scroll of its bark

QUESTION

Body my house
my horse my hound
what will I do
when you are fallen

Where will I sleep
How will I ride
What will I hunt

Where can I go
without my mount
all eager and quick
How will I know
in thicket ahead
is danger or treasure
when Body my good
bright dog is dead

How will it be
to lie in the sky
without roof or door
and wind for an eye

With cloud for shift
how will I hide?

THE GREATER WHITENESS

On winter white
  the dead are gray
    In summer night
      the dead were oh so white
        Upon their grief-wet burial day
          the dead were black against the clay
Oh soiled with grief
  when newly dead
    at foot and head
      in summer's moon-black leaf
        the dead were white
          And in the noon-green
            ghost and stone
              rose clean as light
                and fair as bone
Oh they were black the heavy dead
  that now are light
    and nothing lack
      But even they
        cannot stay
          Oh cannot be
            white as that winter purity
On winter white
  the dead are gray

I WILL LIE DOWN

I will lie down in autumn
let birds be flying

Swept into a hollow
by the wind
I'll wait for dying

I will lie inert unseen
my hair same-colored
with grass and leaves

Gather me
for the autumn fires
with the withered sheaves

I will sleep face down
in the burnt meadow
not hearing the sound of water
over stones

Trail over me cloud
and shadow
Let snow
hide the whiteness of my bones

RUSTY AUTUMN

Rusty autumn to your breast again I come   Memorial tears
I leave in tarnished spoons of grass
Hold me Mother though I am grown and you are old
and burning only for death

Sky my childhood   Oh familiar blue cobbled with clouds
and misting now as with a cataract
where has Father gone   the abundant laughter
our tent and shelter   broad shoulders of the sun?
My dad my tall my yellow-bright ladder of delight

Rusty autumn on your flat breast I lie
and rocks and ragweed my ribs feel in the shaggy field
A blemish on each beam of stubble
and its slanting lash of shadow   These are spears
that were your milk-soft breast I trod in the upright green
Summer's flesh lay all the years between
and hid the bloom of hate
seeded that other time the horizontal world heaved
with my tears   Now too late for planting

Oh mummied breast Oh brown Mother hold me
though you are cold   and I am grown   grown old

GREEN RED BROWN AND WHITE

Bit an apple on its red
side   Smelled like snow
Between white halves broken open
brown winks slept in sockets of green

Stroked a birch white as a thigh
scar-flecked smooth as the neck
of a horse   On mossy pallets green
the pines dropped down
their perfect carvings brown

Lost in the hairy wood
followed berries red
to the fork   Had to choose
between green and green   High

in a sunwhite dome a brown bird
sneezed   Took the path least likely
and it led me home   For

each path leads both out and in
I come while going   No to and from
There is only here   And here
is as well as there   Wherever
I am led I move within the care
of the season
hidden in the creases of her skirts
of green or brown or beaded red

And when they are white
I am not lost   I am not lost then
only covered for the night

AN OPENING

Close to sleep an Opening
    What was wall
    to the light-filled eye
    or panel fingertips could find no groove in
    slides apart
    The Box of Now of Me of only Here unlocks

At once in a landscape limitless and free
    all that my Eye encircles I become
    Trees ponds pastures bullocks grazing there
    silks of my Skin strands of my Hair
    waters of my Body glittering

Then and Forever are my two hands spread
    forgotten by each other
    my Head an orchard where in noons of ebony
    in the white night are mated East and West
    and polar fruits and flowers from the sea
    are harvested together

Now I know I have been Hooded
    On rails my sight has run
    to its Horizon where the future spun
    or tapered to the gray Thread hooked in the past
    And these have dropped away
    like markers lost in corridors of Snow
    I am an eye that without socket looks
    on all sides above below

Where is Wakeness then?
    Rigid these wires and joints and jerky stilts
    when Upright I am stretched in the frame again
    the sky a Lid I cannot pry
    the air a tissue of whispers I cannot tear

When narrowed utterly the final Blind
    box of sleep clapped shut
    unhinged from sight then will I find
    within the pupil of the total deep the Wide
    doorway to fields of Bright
    bristles of the sun to be my hide?

Index of Titles

MAY SWENSON was born in Logan, Utah, of Swedish parents who became American citizens. Her childhood environment was small town rural; she graduated from what was then Utah State Agricultural College. After a year as a reporter on a Salt Lake City daily, she came to New York City. She has worked as author's assistant, editor, reviewer, occasional teacher and poet-in-residence. May Swenson has contributed to numerous national and literary magazines, some of her short stories have been anthologized, and a play, *The Floor*, has been produced at the American Place Theatre, New York City. Since 1954 she has published eight volumes of poems, and has translated the work of the Swedish poet Tomas Tranströmer. May Swenson is a member of the American Academy and Institute and the recipient of many awards and grants. She lives at Sea Cliff, New York.